one-way ticket

WHAT'S BEEN SAID ABOUT SOME OF THE OTHER COTEAU BOOKS TITLES BY ROBERT CURRIE

Running in Darkness (poetry)
"Enthusiastically recommended reading for anyone who appreciates the breadth and depth of contemporary poetry, *Running in Darkness* is a collection of Canadian poet Robert Currie's latest work. Deftly crafted free verse expressions embedded with imagination, imagery, cadence, irony, perception, humour, genuine affection and occasional loss."

– THE MIDWEST BOOK REVIEW

The Days Run Away (poety)
"Like Al Purdy and Alden Nowlan – both of whom make appearances here – Currie writes in plain language, the diction and cadences of ordinary people as they work to understand a world at once heartbreaking and joyful. Those already familiar with Currie's body of work will find him in fine form; those new to his epiphanic poetry will discover a strong introduction to an important prairie voice."

– THE MALAHAT REVIEW

Things You Don't Forget (short stories)
"In Robert Currie's *Things You Don't Forget*, a new and splendid collection of 11 short stories, nobility of spirit is dramatically pitted against the realities of existence... [This] is to my mind the best book of stories published in Canada in the past decade. It's a memorable accomplishment, one that makes you impatient to read more."

– THE TORONTO STAR

Teaching Mr. Cutler (novel)
"*Teaching Mr. Cutler* is (Currie's) first novel and it's a dandy... It's one thing for a teacher to make a lesson exciting for a class of students, but it's quite another for a writer to make a lesson exciting for a reader, and Currie succeeds admirably."

– WINNIPEG FREE PRESS

one-way ticket

Robert Currie

COTEAU BOOKS

Edited by Dave Margoshes
Designed & typeset by Susan Buck
Cover art by Wilf Perreault, "Alley Treats", 1999, acrylic on canvas, 152.4 x 152.4 cm
Printed and bound in Canada

Library and Archives Canada Cataloguing in Publication

Currie, Robert, 1937-, author
One-way ticket / Robert Currie.
Poems.

Issued in print and electronic formats.
ISBN 978-1-55050-952-6 (softcover).--ISBN 978-1-55050-953-3 (PDF)
I. Title.
PS8555.U7O54 2018 C811'.54 C2018-902744-4 C2018-902745-2

COTEAU BOOKS

2517 Victoria Avenue
Regina, Saskatchewan
Canada S4P 0T2
www.coteaubooks.com

Available in Canada from:
Publishers Group Canada
2440 Viking Way
Richmond, British Columbia
Canada V6V 1N2

10 9 8 7 6 5 4 3 2 1

Coteau Books gratefully acknowledges the financial support of its publishing program by: the Saskatchewan Arts Board, The Canada Council for the Arts, the Government of Saskatchewan through Creative Saskatchewan, the City of Regina. We further acknowledge the [financial] support of the Government of Canada. Nous reconnaissons l'appui [financier] du gouvernement du Canada.

This book and this poem are for Gwen.

UNEXPECTEDLY

I steer the car into our driveway,
crunch of snow under the tires.
I lug my bags toward the house, breeze
on my neck like a snowman's breath.

An abrupt call, a single syllable, "Hi,"
and I turn back to the street, a woman walking
in a long black parka, fur-trimmed hood
shadowing her eyes, and I'm struck

by her smile, the same one
I've known for over half a century,
the smile that delights me now
when a greeting restores me to you,

surprised again by the rush I feel
whenever we meet merely by chance.

Table of Contents

"We're all born with a one-way ticket..."
—Charles Wright

The past, remembered

MEMORIES OF TEMPLE GARDENS
(1921–1978)

Buddy Knox said it first: "Rock 'n' roll in Canada
started at Temple Gardens in Moose Jaw."
In the 50s he rocked the room with the Rhythm Orchids,
"Party Doll" and "Hula Love" blasting from the speakers.
We all remember jiving, slow-dancing, the Crickets,
the Champs on the bandstand, big stars in town,
Gene Pitney, and Conway Twitty before he went country,
that cool Canadian kid, Bobby Curtola and "Fortune Teller,"
teens caught and swirled, a whirlwind of Curtolamania
before the Beatles crossed the Atlantic.

Some folks still talk about the night Don Messer
and his Islanders drew sixteen hundred dancers,
the hall packed too tight for dancing, the best
hardwood floor in Western Canada wasted.
Others remember how it felt to swing, Bobby Gimby
on his soaring trumpet, the Tommy Dorsey Orchestra,
or Mart Kenney and his Western Gentlemen.
There was honey on the moon that night,
a few old folks recalling the sweet melodies
of Cal Temple's Tantalizing Toe Ticklers,

but what I remember best are Joe and the Dynamics,
the band spread across the front of the stage,
slashing away at electric guitars,
each of them moving in unison, swinging
their legs left and right, boots as high as their belts,
and there we were in front of them, all of us,
kicking like a line of spastic Rockettes.

"Tramples," we called the place, and after that
it was a convention centre for the Grant Hall Hotel,
then a bingo hall, the target for a wrecking ball,
and Joni Mitchell got it right, a bit of paradise
knocked down to make a parking lot.

ABOVE AND BELOW

I was forty-eight before I flew in a plane
but sometimes before that I floated at night
and hovered over homes where our family once lived:

609 Main South in Moose Jaw, the guys and I
with shovels and boards creating a backyard cave,
our shadows below stretching like miners at work;

302 31st Street in Saskatoon, cement sidewalks,
half a dozen kids hunched over tricycles, pumping hard,
racing, the Tour de Town, a prize for each of us;

the house at the end of the road in Hendon,
me playing with matches in the long grass
and me up above watching the flames catch;

the tin shack by the grain elevator in Furness,
Boots, the family dog, pulling me in the sled
with the apple box coach, me gazing down,

summer now, Boots asleep on the elevator ramp,
a cloud of grain dust, the empty truck kicks into gear,
grinding away from the bin, me floating above,

unable to shout or descend, the truck
picking up speed, a screech of brakes,
the right front wheel bouncing once.

1937

No one knew that the Depression
would ever end when my parents brought me
from the hospital to the two room tin shack
that slouched in the shadow of the UGG elevator
where my father bought whatever grain
the farmers could glean from parched fields.

Beside the door was the box that held wood
for the black metal stove that heated the shack.
On the open shelves of the west wall
my mother's wedding dishes were arranged
by size and carefully stacked upside down.
When the wind blew, as it usually did,
the windows rattled, tin siding howled,
dust stirred on the shelves.
We could taste it, dry and stale in the air.

Outside, twenty steps away, was the outhouse
– its seat like ice on your butt, my father said.
That outhouse blew over in a blizzard so fierce
the snow drifts darkened our windows.
On cold evenings as frost covered
the window panes and worked its way
through the door, spreading along the walls,
I lay in a crib made from a wooden box,
covered by a quilt folded and folded again.

My parents sat close to the stove, blankets
around their shoulders as they read
by the flickering light of a kerosene lamp,
their glances in my direction frequent.
Not until I studied history in high school
would I learn that the Depression was hard
and think that we might have been poor.

HOCKEY DREAMS

I wasn't like him yet, but I was going to be.
The ice at dusk was bright with moonlight,
my skates cutting patterns as I spun
on the goalie, a quick flick of the stick,
backhand shot over his shoulder, winning goal,
the light in my eye flashed red, arms over my head
as I slid into a snow bank. Scoring like him, like Max.

Playing for the Chicago Black Hawks, Max Bentley
was "The Dipsy Doodle Dandy from Delisle."
He could thread a pass through the eye
of a moving needle, stickhandle through a rage
of opponents, make them marvel why
they couldn't smash him, nail him to the boards.
Twice he won the scoring title.

Once he came for supper at our house
(Max's sister was married to my Uncle Lex).
I dressed up so he'd want me for his line mate:
a King Edward School athletic jersey
and my dad's canvas hockey pants.
I looked like Porky Pig in giant bloomers, and that
was as close as I ever got to the NHL.

GROWING UP LUCKY

Sometimes I think of the freedom
my parents extended me as a boy,
the freedom that came with warnings
to be careful, to choose wisely.

So my friends and I camped overnight at Round Hill
when we were in grade six, our sleeping bags
under the open sky, the crescent moon
a shining sickle harvesting stars overhead.
We discovered the wooden snow fences
that guarded the tracks in December
and stacked them in April, making rafts
that rode the current that raged for a week
as soon as the ice went out.
We walked the CN trestle, slight figures
wobbling over the water, our bodies so slim we knew
if we looked down, we'd slip between the ties,
and soon we learned the thrill of crossing the river
by crawling on the girders below, our fingers tight
on black steel and white as pigeon shit on the beams.

And sometimes too I think of the freight train
that fell off the tracks one winter morning,
boxcars and tank cars rolled down the bank,
twisted steel in a smoking wreck, right by the trestle,
exactly where we were playing the day before.

THIEF

I barely had it stuffed in my pocket
when the hand seized my shoulder.
A clerk dragged me to the back of the store,
up half a dozen stairs to the manager's office.
"This boy's a thief," was what she said
when she let me go, my shoulder burning.

"Hand it over," said the manager. "Right now."
He sat at his desk on a wooden chair with wheels,
and he spun toward me, his voice
a rusty spade slicing through gravel.
I dug into my pocket and hauled it out,
my hand shaking, a Roy Rogers cap gun.
"Now, let's have your name and phone number."

I might have lied, but I stammered the truth.
"Come on!" he said. "Speak up so I can hear you."
I could still make up a name, give him the number
of my friend whose parents were never home,
but no, not me, I told the truth a second time.
He whirled back to his desk and dialled.
Oh Lord, my father, he was talking to my father.
When he finished, he wheeled toward me.
"That's that," he said. "You leave this store
and don't come back. Your old man will deal with you."

I got out of there fast, but beyond the outside door
my feet would hardly move, my father waiting at home.
It was already suppertime when I reached the subway
beneath the tracks, but I leaned on the guard rail,
counting every boxcar that rattled overhead.
When finally I dragged myself up the hill and home,
I stood in the backyard, not once glancing at the door
where my father would be waiting. Would he spank me?
I hoped he would. Somehow I knew already,
that when at last I raised my eyes to his,
I'd never forget the look on his face.

THE CHILDREN'S GAME

We played the game on Sundays
when my parents turned up the volume,
engrossed by Mr. DeMille and his Lux Radio Theatre.
Our playing field was the bare basement below,
the coal bin in the far corner, furnace beside it.
My friends and I put cardboard boxes
over our heads and shoulders,
switched off the single bulb
on a basement beam, lowered our heads
and charged one another, rebounded,
bumped something or someone, knocked
something else, slammed into concrete walls,
bounced off the furnace – its pipes quaked and rattled.

At the top of the stairs a sudden light as the door
swung open, the looming shadow of my father.
"You boys, keep it quiet down there. You hear me?"
We waited, breathless and still, for darkness to drop,
then crept away from the furnace and began again.
In the other end of the basement, we attacked, flung
ourselves into the darkness, lunged at every sound,
pounded and battered each other till finally we fell,
panting and spent on the concrete, sweat
on our heaving chests, not understanding why
we so desperately wished the girls from school
could be with us here on the floor.

EVERYTHING WE KNEW

When Kenny and I were twelve we knew everything
about sex. We'd studied the word "friction"
in our *Highroads to Learning School Dictionary*:
"the action of one object rubbing against another,"
and we knew what that meant. We'd seen Rita
Hayworth do the Dance of the Seven Veils in *Salome*,
her body whirling and swaying before King Herod
as the veils dropped away, one delicious veil
after the other, her bosom moving toward us, smooth
and round, so different from the shapes of the girls
at school, who always blushed in health class
and stared down at their desks. Sometimes
Kenny and I would talk in our backyard pup tent
about doing it, about exactly how you would do it,
we'd discuss what it would mean to be in the same bed
as Rita Hayworth without any clothes on.
We were horny and hard in our sleeping bags,
yearning for Rita and her twin sister to join us.
We knew even then we could do something about it
– friction would do the trick – but we understood
the dangers involved: pimples and hair loss,
brain fevers, blindness, and bent peckers.
So we clenched our fists on our chests, wishing
for girls to marry, free at last to give it a try.
But what about girls, we wondered, why
would they put up with it when there was
nothing in it for them?

GODSEND

Danny led me into his parents' bedroom,
both of us on tiptoes though no one was home.
He slid open the top drawer of the dresser
and when he lifted out a pile of sweaters
I caught the faintest whiff of lavender,
the same scent I once smelled mixed with
cinnamon when Mrs. Elliott leaned close
to hand me a sticky bun warm off the counter.

"You won't believe what I found," Danny whispered
as he folded back a plaid skirt and lifted it out,
a foam rubber breast, round
as half a grapefruit, an upright nub
like a real nipple in its exact centre.
I thought of Mrs. Elliott in her purple sweater,
the way her breasts pushed out the cloth.
"You know what?" Danny said. "It's called
a falsie. If you want, you can hold it a sec."

I reached and took it, the nipple's nub
like a living thing in the palm of my hand.
A rattle at the back door. I stuffed
the breast under the skirt, Danny hurling
sweaters into the drawer shoving it shut
and we flung ourselves down the hall
floorboards bouncing and howling back
to his room our breath hammered the wall.

Chest heaving, heart pounding,
I collapsed against the closed door.
I wondered if he'd ever show me
the second falsie. But did it matter?
I already knew exactly how
it would feel in my other hand.

After that I never once looked at Mrs. Elliott
without thinking she must be a bit of a phony.
She was a great mother, always
giving us cookies and stuff – why would she
want to look like a movie star in a sweater?
A week later, I overheard my own mother
whisper to my father that Esther Elliott
was beating the big C, she'd only needed
the one surgery, and that was a godsend.
What was the big C, I wondered,
and what the heck was a godsend?

BECAUSE I NEVER

Because I never learned to dance
I stood fixed in the high school gym,
music blasting around me while I gazed
at the backboard, the hoop, its net
dropping a mesh of shadows on the floor.
I told the guys I could hardly wait
for tomorrow's basketball practice
when what I craved was nerve enough
to walk the empty space in front of me
– like a soldier, upright and brave, reckless,
no doubt, slowly traversing no-man's land –
stepping away from this group of guys
toward that distant line of girls
who laughed and talked so easily together
as if they never noticed when a guy
found a way to cross that vacant floor.
I tried not to stare at the grade eleven girl
who stood fifth from the end of the line, silver
earrings flashing, pony tail bobbing on her shoulder.
I stayed within the shadows of the net
as if held there by a giant spider's web.

Because I never learned to dance
my mother spoke to Mrs. Loveridge
and hired her daughter, Lucrezia,
to teach me how to jive, and for five weeks
every Wednesday after school I descended
to their basement rumpus room, praying
no friend of mine had seen me sneak inside,
and there I tried to beat my feet to the rhythms
of Bill Haley and the Comets, Lucrezia at ease
and liquid in my arms, stepping perfectly, whirling
when I threw her out with one hand, caught her
with the other, spinning her behind my back,
twirling her beneath my arm, me already fearing
what I knew was bound to be the truth,
I'd never learn to dance
with any other girl.

BEST YEAR

My year in grade twelve, Central Collegiate, room 4A:
the eyes of the guys at the front move
with Nancy Beamish as she glides into the room,
it's like the opening scene of a stage play.
I sit in the desk behind Marilynn Carefoot
who sometimes turns to me, her smile incandescent.
Inky Sinclair, three rows over and one seat back,
claims he can fart whenever he wants.
When Carol Dobney asks him to prove it,
Inky says, "But right now I don't want to,"
Sam Yamakami snorting into his history text.
Launched like a nervous actor on opening night,
Chuck Lyon forgets to begin his speech
with a proper address to the class,
but quickly recovers: "Friends, Romans,
Countrymen, lend me your ears."
Clink Mackay swears he can get his father's truck
and tonight we'll cruise the Main drag till midnight.
Searce Searcy tells us that Val Hergesheimer's
bra strap came undone in period three
and you could almost see her nipple,
but he doesn't tell us till period four.
Chenny Chow has hockey cards on his desk
of both Maurice "The Rocket" Richard
and his brother Henri, "The Pocket Rocket,"
but on the far side of the room we've got
Boris Romanchych who can handle a hockey stick too,
and we call him Bor – eece, "The Jock Pocket Rocket."
Mr. Robinson is reading the graveyard scene from Hamlet,
and sobs echo across the room – Pam Marshall
in the cloak room, crying, her boyfriend gone.
In Latin class, Searce supplies for Mr. Morrow

a new and lively version of "Horatio at the Bridge,"
Horatio being a pig farmer from south of town
who stampedes his herd of pigs across the bridge,
which collapses into the Tiber River just in time
to save Rome from a horde of barbarian invaders,
and we're convulsed by his performance.
Fuzz Shaw is class president and quarterback
of the football team, and when I say
I sure hope I make the team this year
he laughs and says he knows I will,
and events roll out like a movie script:
on my very first play at defensive end
I manage to nail the runner for a big loss.
Mr. Chapman is reviewing homework in chem lab,
and for once I know the answer, but he asks
Pooner Lawson, who says, "Carbon monoxide,"
Mr. Chapman wheeling around, heading
for the detention book on his desk. "No,"
hollers Pooner, "it's carbon dioxide. Carbon *dioxide*!"
"Sorry, George," says Mr. Chapman. "Only one guess."
and even Pooner chuckles at that.
It's our last year in high school, and I've finally
figured a few things out, I've got a nickname at last,
and I want it all to go on forever, but already
Fuzz and Searce, Pooner and Sam
are accepted for Engineering at the U of S,
Nancy's boyfriend is planning to give her a ring,
Chenny's set for pre-med and Marilynn for music ed,
and somewhere, down along Main Street,
or off on the west side of town, the site
of lumber yards and construction firms,
I know somehow I've got to find me a job.

HEAVY HITTER

What was it like to be Masayuki Yamakami,
my Japanese friend from grade three through twelve?
In the war years he and his whole family
were interned somewhere out past the airport,

though none of us kids knew about that. Later they moved
into town, his father starting a dry-cleaning shop on River Street,
his sisters practicing piano, becoming so good
every soloist in town wanted to work with them,

and Mas – or Sam as we called him then
in our nicknaming days – could slam a soft ball
so hard it would fly so high over the outfield
it would land on the roof of King Edward School.

Sam passed through town once in the 90s.
Checking messages, I heard his name, his voice
on our answering machine; going through
to Winnipeg, sorry to miss you, was all that he said.

But there he was in his Central Celtics jacket
for our 50th anniversary class reunion,
Sam, immediately recognizable as himself,
the happiest, youngest-looking guy in the group.

And by then I had some idea of how his family
had been carted off from their homes in B.C.,
their lands and boats seized, everything
they owned taken away, loyal Canadians

labelled enemy aliens, and how did he do it,
my old school friend, who somehow managed
to be the most popular kid in our class
while his classmates collected war comics

and dreamed of killing Nazis and Japs?

THAT SUMMER WITH CHARLIE

The summer I needed money for college
I hit every construction office in town
and finally got my chance, a new motel
going up three miles east on the highway, be there
by eight and they'd find me something to do.
My dad bought me a pair of steel-toed boots
and the next morning drove me out to the job site.
The foreman put me with Charlie, a little guy
with the strength of a Clydesdale horse.
His grip, when we shook, was callus and grit.
He was good with power tools and hammers,
good with cement, with tampers
and edgers, bull floats and trowels,
had me sweating to keep up with him.

Charlie drove down Coteau Street every morning,
picked me up at the corner close to our house,
telling me stories about what it was like
to be a soldier in the war, and how much
those Dutch girls loved the Canadian guys,
Charlie with the window always open,
cigarette spraying ashes over his shirt.
Once, when laying a pad of cement
for the long line of motel rooms, it meant
overtime for some of the crew, and Charlie
told the boss that I always rode with him,
I might as well stay; thirteen hours we worked,
it would be the biggest payday of my life.

Afterwards, driving home with Charlie at dusk,
I kept dozing off in the passenger seat, Charlie
tapping my shoulder at the corner, grinning
and telling me, "Don't forget, tomorrow morning
I'll pick you up the same time as usual,"
Charlie who died a dozen years ago,
and not till I read his obit in the paper
did I think of our long gone summer together,
and realize how stupid I was, the kid
who never once thought to chip in for gas.

SUMMER JOB

The seconds crept by like minutes
on their hands and knees, me labouring
for Inland Construction on the motel job,
my lonely task one endless day
wiring rebar in place, metal ribs
to reinforce the concrete they'd pour
tomorrow for the office basement.
My hands in gloves were wet with sweat,
pliers twisting wire to bind the steel,
my mind somewhere else, a hummingbird
that hovered here and there, then was gone.
I thought of this and that and everything:
– the April day we kids swam bareballs
in the creek, the water so cold we knew
there must be ice just around the bend;
– the girl who sat ahead of me at school,
peach fuzz on the neck I yearned to touch;
– the horses we rode last summer,
each of us afraid not to take a turn
on the old roan that bucked;
– the beer we drank the day we learned
we'd all passed every College final;
– that magazine photo of steel workers on a girder,
a casual line of them, lunch boxes open,
their feet dangling high above Manhattan;
– and me in a basement excavation trying
to pretend I had a job that made me a guy
some girl somewhere would admire.

SUMMER OF FREEDOM

Four young guys in a basement suite in the city,
on lazy evenings like gophers out of our burrow
we'd rise to take the sun on the step, sipping our beer,
talking of the girls we knew – or wanted to know.

Some mornings when no one would concede
it was his turn to mop the floors this week,
we'd stand on chairs to pull on our pants,
fuzz waiting to cling to our cuffs.

Our usual supper began with a pot of boiling water,
two cans of beans, holes punched in the top,
the cans adrift, eight eggs bobbing around them,
and when the beans were hot, the eggs hard-boiled,
we'd pour the water into cups for instant coffee,
a little saved for scalding the dishes clean.

Fred one night, while frying hamburger,
spilled meat on the floor, walked through it
as he worked at the stove and the counter,
the kitchen linoleum like pavement and roadkill.

The following night we settled on pizza,
and planned a party for the labour-day weekend,
a party that three of us thought worth the scrubbing.
The girls we invited, they arrived at last,
and we toured them through Fred's room:

to the left of the bed, his dirty clothes
ankle deep on the floor, and to the right
in a pile nearly as deep, strewn from
the dry cleaner's bag, a heap of clean clothes,
and the girls, they were charmed,
yes, and oh so eager to meet him.

AFTER OUR PHARMACY FINALS *

It was a different world out there
when we came down from Canada that May,
some of us planting our feet in the stirrups,
mounting up at the Saddlebar in Minneapolis, Minnesota,
women dancing before us in fewer and fewer clothes,
peckers hard in our pants, the pharmacy girls shaking
their heads at the open door.
                                        Time to move on,
and we did the next day, the chartered bus
packed for the trip, eight of us in every hotel room,
cots jammed together, Zylich, whose father
ran the King George in Saskatoon, tossing
wet towels on the bathroom floor,
Ed waiting till he was out of the room
before he retrieved them and hung them
neatly back on the rack,
                                        next a college tour, nothing
compared to that night's revelation of a Hawaiian bar
installed here in the middle of Madison, Wisconsin,
exotic women, their hypnotic dance mesmerizing
till Bobby Ortynski hauled his piano accordion up on stage,
grass skirts swaying in sensual delight, a salute to his nerve,
audience cheering an Aloha Ukrainian Hawaiian Polka Fest.
                                        Orange juice
and vodka for breakfast, cheeseburgers
for the rest of our meals, the bus barreling south
on a song, everyone with his own verse,
    Hey li lee, li lee, li lee,
    I'm from Moose Jaw, north of here,
    Hey li lee, li lee, lo,
    we don't do dope, but we sure drink beer,
wild applause, a radio on, making history together,

Alan Shepard, the first American launched into space,
and we blasted on and on through Illinois, Indiana,
to Indianapolis at last, meals and rooms free, courtesy
of Eli Lilly and Company, pristine lab displays, demonstrations,
every bar in town playing "The Peppermint Twist."

Now it was queen-size beds in the Hilton Hotel, four
to a room, it was banquet meals in an elegant ballroom, a slab
of meat three inches thick on my plate, and what was that,
I wondered, was it the "Filet Mignon" on the menu card by my cup,
and who could I ask? Should I try the twelve year old kid
who seemed to inhabit the hall by our rooms? Booze
he offered to bring us at any hour of the day or night.
Always after our cash. He'd prefer, he said,
folding money to spare change, but he'd take it all,
he didn't mind the weight in his jeans, and sure,
he could tell me, the word is "filly," he said, and she
comes in a black garter belt and tits out to here.
I told him to bugger off, but he thought he could tempt us
and wouldn't leave. She was the hottest woman in town,
she could haul your ashes and heat 'em again, and he,
personally, would take us one by one to her room.
When we boarded
the bus for home, he was there, hanging around,
jacket pockets clinking with bottles, his palm up,
a shrewd and lewd look on his face; a few of us
edged by him, refusing to meet his eyes,
and pushed through to the back of the bus.

* The bi-annual visit to Indianapolis for University of Saskatchewan pharmacy students was paid for by The Eli Lily Drug Company, but the students had to pay to get there.

BLIND DATE

When he remembered that night
he thought of his own nervous confusion,
a friend lining up girls for him and his buddy,
and how would he know what to say,
and which one was meant for him?
The first there already, the other riding a bus
home from Saskatoon, they gave her time
to get ready, then drove to her parents' place.
She spilled out of the front door fast, slid
into the seat beside him, and passed her friend
a mickey of gin – the last she'd heard
they'd be watching a movie, drinking alone,
not dancing the New Year in—and he thought
maybe he could manage this, she might be okay,
a girl not afraid to buy her own booze.
Their gang at the dance hall happy and raucous,
the long table covered with bottles and glasses,
four chairs propped against the table for them,
two couples paired up together the first time ever.
This girl, the one who seemed to be with him,
had a smile like the crescent moon seen
from the bed by his window – it compelled
him to gaze – and she wanted to dance,
something he had doubts he could do,
but a couple of drinks and the music
prompted a weird kind of loose-jointed shuffle,
which he could almost execute. He held her
in his arms, his feet apart, not tramping on hers;
she was easy to talk to, he didn't blather at all,
and should he worry about taking her home,

what to do at the front step on a first date?
Midnight coming, it might be all right,
everyone here singing "Auld Lang Syne,"
and he bent slowly toward her, their lips
touching, and she was kissing him back.

THE HUNTER

When I was ten I wished I was Pork
who earned his fame in the field by Round Hill,
his homemade hickory bow strung and raised,
his eye on the mound where a gopher stood at attention.
He notched the arrow, pulled the string on a slow line
to his chin. Held his breath and released.
The arrow sliced through the gopher's belly,
through the neck of another unseen behind.
Two dead with one shot, his glory assured.

When I was fifteen I spent a winter day
with Roger walking the hills and coulees east of town,
our twenty-two rifles gripped in gloved hands.
Every half hour or so a jackrabbit would conjure itself
from the snow and bounce off, our rifles blasting behind.
A chill return to town, wind drawing tears from our eyes,
my finger too numb to find the trigger, another jack
bounded before us, and Roger shot twice,
a blossom of blood on white fur. Jealousy
like a flame that burned off the cold.

Hunting with Al at thirty-five, I rose
from the brush, swung the borrowed shotgun
in the flight-path of the mallard, gauged his speed
and fired, the bird collapsing, tumbling
to the edge of the slough. A thrill
up my spine like nothing I'd known before.
I picked up the bird, wings hanging, gorgeous
green feathers on the dangling head.
Its body warm. But not for long. A dead thing.
When I dropped it into the sack with Al's kill,
I knew I'd regret forever the fellowship
gone, but I was done with hunting.

WALKING WITH FUZZ

Back at my old high school after ten years,
I stand before my first class, faces not exactly
hostile, but immobile, blank, impossible to read,
and for some reason I recall walking with Fuzz.

It was grade twelve after a sleep-over at his place,
kit-bags over our shoulders, on our way
to the armoury for Saturday basketball practice.
Little kids kept appearing beside us,
popping their heads over fences, darting
out of back alleys and front doors.
"Hi, Dick," they said. "Hey, Dick."
One of them even called him, "Mr. Shaw."
Their eyes wide as pucks, their faces
shining like the ice inside a goalie's crease.
Fuzz who was five foot six, but quarterback
of the football team, slapped them
on the shoulders, spoke to them all,
and I thought what a shame, him the best
hockey player in town, the city rink
burned down and the hockey team gone
just when he's hitting his stride,

and these students frozen in front of me,
were some of them the ones who worshipped him,
and how would they think of me
when our year together was done?

ONE OF THOSE DAYS

Literature class, last class of a bad day,
kids more interested in the moving hand
of the clock than anything I have to say.
The bell rings and they're off, scrambling
for the door, the first signs of animation
since the end of the previous class.
If I blocked their way, would they trample me?
Would they even notice I was there? Maybe,
but I wonder, is this just a waste of time?

A phone call at nine that night. From Jim,
a boy in grade ten, who says he needs to talk.
Words pitch and tumble, never a stop for breath.

"That book you told me to try, I can hardly believe it.
Lennie, they were going to hunt him down like a dog,
shoot him or lynch him. Sure, he killed Curley's wife,
but it was an accident, he didn't mean it.
But George finds Lennie first and he tells him
their old story about the farm – they're gonna buy it together.
What he's doing, he's trying to make Lennie feel better,
and George, he pulls out a gun and shoots him dead,
so he can die happy. I just had to tell you.
In my whole life it's the best book I ever read."

WHAT I THINK OF WHEN I THINK OF ROBIN HOOD

Sunday evening, the dark school, lights
in the old auditorium, students bursting
with fervour, it's not quite the final rehearsal,
but they've become actors, getting their lines
right, or almost right, ad libbing as needed,
the pacing smooth, that artless flow of energy,
all but the boy who drags his dejection over the stage,
dropping lines, a glum frown aimed in my direction.
"Come on, Ross," I say. "You look like your best friend
just died. Get into character. You're better than this."
He flashes a sullen scowl but picks up his next cue.

The Monday paper tells about Saturday night.
The name not yet released of the boy
possessed by thoughts no adult can share,
the boy who clung to the side of the Robin Hood mill
for how long, Lord, before he made up his mind?
I learn at school today he was Ross's friend,
and I try not to picture the boy on the ground,
broken, bones fractured, skull shattered,
the splatter of blood that Ross saw or imagined,
and still he came out to work on our play.

That Sunday evening, how could I have possibly known
what I was saying, and why couldn't I have just
kept my stupid mouth shut?

AT THE HIGH SCHOOL REUNION

We teachers were seated together
on bleachers, former students waiting
to greet us, a hush in the gym.
When the man with the mic said it was time
to meet the staff, there was a rush
across the floor. The woman who darted
toward me was dark-haired, pretty, wore an easy smile,
was, she said, pleased to see me again,
my classes were always worthwhile.

I would have recognized her, but I was sure
I'd never seen her before, and I told her
I'd certainly know if I'd ever taught her.
She stepped back, her eyes brittle as glass
– I ought to have lied, but I'd been nineteen years
at the school, knew every student in my every class.
Then a sudden thought: "Were you in Mr. Knuttila's room
when he was off a month and I took over for him?"

She shook her head, half-lowered it, stood
like a distant relative at a grave-side service,
waiting for the priest to finish his spiel
so she could leave the deceased behind
and resume the business of life.
                                        What an arrogant fool
I was to argue with her. A former student spurned.
I should have grabbed her sleeve when she turned away
and spun her around. Apologized. She knew
who her teacher was, and I, her teacher,
had not one clue.

HOOKED

When my dad was drying dishes,
he'd hook his cane in his back pocket,
one hip cocked higher than the other
as he leaned over the sink for a plate.
The plate dry, he'd hitch himself toward the table
and add another to the stack of shining dishes.
It was arthritis, but he never complained.
At work he always hung his cane
on the right-hand corner of the desk
while he filled the ledgers of the Livestock Pool,
but the cane dangled, swinging, from his pocket
when we played catch in the yard at home.

When I was in high school,
rushing from the Uptown Cafe,
my new friends and I howling at some joke
that one of the guys had just made up,
there he was, my dad, crossing the street,
the light already red, my dad trying to hurry,
his cane striking the pavement, thunk, thunk,
as he jerked himself toward the curb.
I told my friends I had to go,
then turned and walked the other way.

YOU LOVING ME

Steel-toed boots, size nine, leather worn
and cracked, under a layer of dust,

they sit on my parents' basement floor
beneath a shelf of paint cans and jars,

next to a row of sandals and shoes,
sit where they've sat for years,

the boots you never wore to the office,
the boots you refused to throw out.

Once when the cutbacks came, your job
suddenly as secure as a roof under a wrecking ball,

you said, "If bad gets to worse,
I can always work construction.

I've got the boots for the job. No need
to sweat it, son. We're gonna be fine."

HIS PRESENCE

As important as your own bank account,
he said to me, every boy should have one.
My father's jackknife with the worn blade,
the one he used for years at the office,
sharpening pencils to a point as precise
as the figures he wrote in his ledger,
I kept it for years in my sweater pocket,
the sweater I wore for warmth in the archives,
sharpening my own pencils, their points
carefully carved in memory of him.

Often while writing at the long table
my hand dropped of its own accord
into that pocket, my fingers wrapping
around that pearl handle, solid,
like my father's grip on my shoulder
when he thought I'd need cheering.

My sweater draped over a chairback
while I walked outside in the heat of noon,
I returned to the archives and dipped my hand
into the pocket. Found it empty. Nothing
but a bit of lint in one corner.

My father suddenly as distant
as a hill on the far horizon,
a lone coyote howling
at a fading moon.

SAVING THE FISH

I lean over the river, water sluggish in summer,
a sunlit shimmer that shows me a boy, skinny,
his bomber jacket too big for his shoulders.
He's bent over with a pail in his hands, scooping
up fish where the ice is broken, where water
slides between rocks at the shallow spot,
some of the rocks laid there by the boy
to make a stable crossing into the woods,

the rocks like a dam then, frantic fish gasping
and flopping, beating themselves on the rocks,
the boy with the pail of fish lugging them
downstream to where he's chopped a hole
in the ice, his driven task to deliver the fish,
release them into deeper water, then run
back to scoop up as many more as he can,
his pants crusted with ice,
the boy out of breath, legs shaking
from the strain of running, but refusing
to pause, carrying pail after pail,

the boy who must've been me, and what relation
is he to the man leaning over the water a moment,
then slowly turning to shuffle along the paved walk
by this same river, the man shuffling
because his left knee is stitched with pain
when he hurries, the man having forgotten
till now that boy desperate to save all the fish
which the man knows were nothing but suckers.

Inspiration, everywhere

BACK ALLEY MAN

for Wilf Perreault

A derelict car tilts into the darkening lane,
flat tires on two wheels, a puddle infused
with waning light from the evening sky,
the heavens caught between drifts of snow
here where he strolls, picking his way
between watery ruts and garbage cans,
their lids topped by sloppy white tuques,
telephone poles laying quilt-like shadows
across the path that draws him in.

He thinks of his childhood in Saskatoon,
walking back alleys with his father,
the closeness they felt, their eyes
on the ground, the sudden thrill of light
thrown back from glass in the weeds,
another beer bottle to add to their sack.

He imagines a palette in his hand, paints
to catch the green fence that leans
into a drift, a blue glow on the snow, paints
to play with light from the glimmering sky,
a single bulb in the window of a dark garage,
a dim moon rising between silhouettes of elms,
years to discover patterns in snow, gravel, mud,
to capture their textures, beauty in the ordinary.
He knows already he wants to die
with a paintbrush in his hand.

FUR TRADERS DESCENDING THE MISSOURI

after George Bingham

The boy leans on a bale of furs
and dreams of the panorama downstream,
ladies in gowns at a steamboat rail,
passengers beginning to disembark,
the bustle of workers on the quay
where carriages are drawn by fine horses,
their hooves the size of chopping blocks,
manes and tails braided with ribbons.
Sights his Indian mother will never see.

His father smokes a pipe, his paddle
plying the smooth river, the current
pulling their canoe past a jutting rock
that draws a line in the water
as true as a nib follows a straight-edge.
Behind them clumps of bush on an island,
trees on the far shore vague in the haze.
Wide river under the vast Montana sky.

Chained at the front of the log canoe
is a strange creature, a dog or cat,
perhaps, or a wild animal tamed,
its shadow expanding over the water,
but the creature is still, at ease with its masters.
Pipe smoke white as a dove's breast feathers the air.

All three gaze with calm regard at the viewer
who longs for the rough feel of the paddle,
who would step over the painting's frame
and risk a seat by the beast in the prow,
who would ride down that huge brown river.
The scene serene as his dream of the past.

THE SCENE ON CAROL STREET

after Ben Shahn

Far down the block the women tramp,
practical footwear black on pavement,
a street the colour of scabs and blood.
They brandish fists, wave their hands
toward the long red building, craving,
calling for, demanding decent wages.
Like a fortress wall the office building
stretches a long block down the long street.
No entrance, not a door in sight.

A double row of closed windows
behind which a few men loiter,
white shirts, rolled sleeves, they have
their own concerns, profit margins,
ways to limit extra pay for overtime.
At the window farthest from the women
another boss lounges against the casement,
his chin resting in his cupped hand.
Not a glance toward the hapless women.
What empty-headed fools, he thinks,
when will they learn to know their place?

THE MISTRESS

after William Holman Hunt

The shapely young woman has been given so much –
rooms in a mansion, rich carpets and draperies,
an exotic clock trimmed with mourning nymphs,
tall mirrors in which to admire her beauty,
the luxuriously coloured shawl wrapped
around her gown with its border of lace,
a pet cat to charm her through empty hours,
the piano with its gleaming finish, its delicate filigree,
on which she picks out tunes overheard in her youth –
all gifts from her jaunty Victorian lover who lolls
in his chair, the fingers of his left hand idly
tapping piano keys, his other hand reaching
around her thigh as she strives to rise from his lap.
She looks somewhere far off, perhaps outside
to the garden, where she might have run
and laughed had she known such a place
as a child, her eyes staring and wide
with sudden comprehension, the cat at play
on the floor, pawing a wounded bird.

CAPE COD EVENING

after Edward Hopper

The man in rolled sleeves sits on the step
of the summer house, looking glum.
He leans down, reaches for the crumpled paper
in the dry grass that rises above his ankles
and surrounds the house like a yellow rash.
Is there a message here he needs to conceal?

The woman stands a few feet away, buttocks
braced on a window frame, her arms hugging
her stomach as if to ward off a chill.
Eyes staring, she seems to survey
nothing but thoughts that trouble her mind.
Does she hear the ominous tapping
of branches on the window beside her?

A few yards away in longer grass, a collie
stands, ears cocked and listening. He turns
his head and waits, muscles bunched, ready.
Behind the house the dark trees disappear
in purple shadows, only their trunks visible
in the dull grass, stalkers cloaked in shadows,
the distant sky black as soot. Something
more than the night approaches.

KING UZZIAH SITS FOR HIS PORTRAIT

after Rembrandt

In the shadows behind the great king
we glimpse the faintest flashes of gold,
hints of splendour, of royal wealth.
His turban of shining silk is graced
by a radiant jewel at the forehead.
A velvet cloak almost covers his vest
of silver, the cloak held on the shoulders
by the elaborate jeweled clasp
gleaming on his chest, pomp
to adorn the portrait of a king.

Extended from flowing sleeves,
the king's left hand is cupped
gracefully in the other, rugged
hands, skin lined and rough.
On the king's cheeks are blotches,
the skin of his nose uneven and gnarled,
unsmiling lips clenched firmly together.
From deep in their furrowed sacks
his eyes stare out, not at the painter,
Uzziah seeing the future he fears,
his lesions untouched by royal decrees,
his ancient, impotent eyes, dull and forlorn.

HOLY CRAP

I see it, sonofabitch,
but I can't believe it,
my grade twelve English teacher
– Mrs. West, the one my buddy claims
should be a funeral director –
she whirls from the chalkboard
and steps up onto her chair,
stands there a second
slowly surveying us all
as if sizing us up for coffins.
Then she leaps onto her desk
and starts to dance – yeah, tap dancing –
her arms outstretched, hands
floating like trained birds
above her head, hair swirling,
as she spins three times,
her dress twirling around – get this –
movie star legs – unbelievable!
toes and heels beating a crescendo
on the desk top before she stops suddenly,
the room silent, all of us startled, breathless,
waiting for her to speak. "Now," she says,
"now that I've got your attention,
the assignment's due a week from Monday,
an essay on Hamlet's tendency toward
procrastination, something everyone
of you should understand."

The opening two lines are from Jim McLean's "C.P.R. Hungarian Rhapsody" in *The Secret Life of Railroaders*.

SOLITARY MAN

Karaoke never paid the rent,
but sometimes it gets rid of his tension,
the frustrations of a bad day, saving
some sap from having his noggin split,
a sharp word, a hard fist to the cheekbone.
Not as satisfying as a head butt
or a swift knee in the nuts, but a song

– well, he does like to sing, "Crackling Rosie"
springing from his lips sweeter than Neil Diamond
ever sang it, shoulders loose now and swaying,
hips beginning to swing, the bar gone quiet,
the poor men's ladies up from their tables,
pushing toward him at the mic and he switches
to "Solitary Man," let them see him suffer,

let them think he wants a woman
who won't play around behind him,
him about as lonely as a cat in heat,
every night a different girl reaching out,
touching him, and if she hesitates, he croons
in her ear, oh no, he can't be hurt holding her.
Get her heated up for an hour of delirious love.

Let the hurting run off his shoulders, eh,
and onto hers, long gone is what he needs to be,
tomorrow night another smokey lady, oh man,
yes, she'll move him, groove him, do him,

just let this singer sing his song.
Yet it's always back to the day job,
the basement suite, rent due on Monday.

The opening line is by Jeanette Lynes from "ABBA Down Cold" in *A Woman Alone on the Atikokan Highway*.

WHAT HE WANTS

His body knows what he wants.
Not the girl from his sixteenth winter
who sat beside him in chemistry class,
and stared at the test tubes he filled,
never raising her eyes to his face.
Not the girl he proposed to
the year after college, the girl who said
yes, then went off to Australia,
writing her marvellous letters
till one said she wouldn't be back.
Not the woman he married, the woman
who loved him and stayed
till the children were gone.

His body knows what he needs.
One last walk through the old house
where he lived with his parents:
the kitchen where he dried the dishes
his father washed, while his mother
picked out tunes on the next-room piano;
the bare basement with the plywood sheet
balanced on saw horses where finally
he beat his father at ping pong;
the dining room table where they gathered
together at the warped crokinole board,
wooden discs flicked from flashing fingers;
the narrow hall with the homemade bookcase,
bottom shelf jammed with Hardy Boys mysteries
and Walter Farley's *Black Stallion* books;
and at the end of the hall, his own room,
the desk where he copied Will James' horses,

and the bed with the quilt where he slept at ease
till the wake-up call of his mother's soft voice, the bed
where even now his body might sleep through the night.

The first line is from Gary Hyland's "Body Song to Hypnos" in *The Work of Snow*.

BETTER AND WORSE

I liked myself better
before I became a saint.
Or tried to become one,
my face bland as a table top,
my voice controlled and mellow,
launching a fleet of cliches,
sharing the news that all is well.
Enough to make a do-gooder puke.

But let us be fair to everyone,
let us be generous without fault,
without hatred or malice, without guile.
Yes. My features calm as an old sock.
Thoughts roiling and fierce, a lump
in my gut like a live coal, fingers
aching for a throat to crush.

How do I go on from here, thrust
forward and back, flaring, defiant,
no more like a saint than a rabid dog?
My days dragged down to gumbo
and shit, I wrangle alone and wonder
what's right. How do I deal
with the fever inside, the rages
that tear me to scraps? God knows,
I could use a saint to show me the way.

The first two lines are from Joanne Weber's "Dorothy Day: Annunciation" in *The Pear Orchard.*

NEAR

In the near dark
when she's almost
asleep she feels
cosy and safe,
her body warm,
electric blanket
curled at her chin,
the radio low,
a slow ballad,
a voice she should
know, a woman
who hits the high
notes and holds
them like gems,
nightlight in the hall,
its glow soft as
fresh fallen snow,
sleep approaching
on tiptoe to smooth
her brow, soothing
her now, that lyrical
voice singing of love
and his gentle touch
– his touch, the bed
shaking, clutch
of the heart,
she knows she's
screaming again.

The first two lines are from Sheri Benning's "What It Tastes Like" in *Thin Moon Psalm*.

HIS OWN MAN

The man at the door with a gun
is our son. We haven't seen him in years.
Not since he told us he needed
to stand tall, to be his own man.
He said he'd be moving south, the States,
the land of unlimited opportunities,
him a believer in limitless sky.
One postcard three months after he left.
A desert scene: a single saguaro cactus
against a sinking sun. No return address.
Headed to the top, it said, you'll be proud.
A card that December wishing us
a white Christmas, wishing he could be home
for the holidays. Then eleven years without a word.
No help from Google. Not a trace of him on-line.
A private detective discovered
he'd lived for three years in Gilbert, Arizona,
but had moved on, no forwarding address.
We had to believe he was still alive.

And now we see he is. Pushing
into the house, gun shaking in his hand.
It's him all right, but he looks older than
us, shoulders stooped, face lined and grey.
He tells us he wants money, needs money
now. Can't wait for his inheritance.
We can make the arrangements tomorrow
or he'll disappear again till we're both gone.

Inherit it then, he says, or maybe he'll leave us
dead on the floor. Speed up the process.
It's entirely up to us, what should he do?
A sudden grimace then, and he begins to cry.

The opening sentence is from Brenda Niskala's "Blunt Instrument" in *How to Be a River*.

AFTER MAKING LOVE WE HEAR FOOTSTEPS

from a title by Galway Kinnell

Have our moans awakened the children,
brought them padding down the hall, fists
at their eyes as they rub away sleep?
But no, they're gone into the world, they sleep
down other halls near children of their own.

Is there then a burglar crouched downstairs, frozen,
his muscles beginning to cramp as he prays
what he heard was a woman cry out in her sleep?

Perhaps there are ghosts on the stairs, aroused
at last from that long and boring sleep; heads cocked
to listen, they linger on the landing, and yearn to hear
more sighs and groans, half-remembered sounds
that haunt their memories: ah, what it was to be alive.

Silence, and a soft thump, footsteps again,
footsteps recede outside our bedroom window,
someone walks beneath a waning moon,

and we lie in each other's arms,
knowing the morning news awaits,
ready to fall like a warning upon us.
We hold each other still, but there's
never a way to hold off the day.

NEAR CAVENDISH

Prince Edward Island – and the Anne Shirley dolls
are everywhere, Green Gables a tourist site,
the farmhouse restored; roof, gables, window frames
painted a dark green, walls a shining white.
The perfect backdrop for flaming red braids.
Visitors from Japan fill the living room
where neighbours and fans once held the wake
for author Lucy Maud Montgomery.
The tourists talk of Anne as if she were real,
someone their parents once knew, a person
of historical significance. And perhaps she is.

We find a motel a few kilometers away,
a motel with a barbecue for the use of guests.
As the sun drops away we cook our steaks
and gaze out on a darkening valley,
geese coming low over the hillside,
flock after flock settling in the field below,
a sight that would have taken the breath
of even Lucy Maud, her pen poised
for a moment over another paragraph,
Anne and Gilbert strolling in Balsam Hollow,
Gilbert just about to reach for her hand.

THE ENVOY OF THE COUNT

after Robert Browning

The Duke shows me the painting on the wall,
his last Duchess, someone who could appall
him when she was alive by her desire
to mingle with the common folk, her dire
need for other company; now she's gone,
he seeks a new wife to look down upon.
This condescending Duke has let it slip
that his main interest is not to grip
the girl, but the dowry my master must
provide. A grievous blunder that I trust
he wouldn't want me sharing with the Count.
Now, suddenly, he's ready to dismount
from his high horse. "We'll go together down, sir,"
says he, hoping that I might just infer
he looks on me almost as an equal,
hoping too that I'll never dare to tell
the Count a word about the dreadful fate
of his last wife, an almost perfect mate,
filled with joy, open and friendly to all,
but loath to worship him, that her downfall,
not to mention her utter disregard
for his nine-hundred-years-old name which barred
her from every chance at happiness.
The Duke gave orders – he seemed to confess
he had her put to death. Exactly what
could the Count's daughter expect from him but
misery and heartache if my report
should favour such a marriage? I can thwart
his plans with plain words of truth, or ascribe
to him good designs – perhaps for a bribe.

This arrogant Duke might be made to pay
– I would treasure that – but still I must weigh
the future of the girl against my gain,
consider too that guilt can cause great pain.
Why not reveal him as haughty and cruel,
nothing but a controlling, jealous fool?
Yes, let him choke on dreams of opulence,
let this monster's suffering be intense.

Others, observed

A CARTON OF MILK

"Care to join us?" a woman asks, but I shake my head
and go right on into Safeway. The wife needs milk
for mixing bran muffins, the skim at home just won't do.
Hardly anyone around, I grab a carton of two per cent,
whip through the express line and out the door.
Almost ten after, and I told Beth I'd be home by ten.
Halfway back to the car, something pops, someone
shouts. A shot, it must've been a shot. More
shots. People dropping. Running away. Some guy
is shooting at us. Get down. I land hard, sharp pain
in my knee, try to squeeze into the pavement. Crazy
guy with a gun. Shot after shot. Thank God,
Beth's at home. Pavement
rough against my cheek. Where are the cops?
Why won't somebody stop him? I saw the sign
across the parking lot: Congress on Your Corner.
What the hell is going on? Screams, just screams
now. Nothing else. Lord, the shooting
is finally stopped. I raise my head, look around,
people getting up, a woman wailing, three guys
wrestling, I'm on my hands and knees – no, two guys,
they've got the gunman down – I better get up, people
on the pavement, blood around them, I feel one knee
buckle, guy beside me grabs me. Some of them are dead.
I hold his arm. Tight. Hear a voice. "Walked right up
to Giffords. Son of a bitch. Shot her in the forehead."
Sirens somewhere now. Guy beside me says, "Maybe
we should sit you down." I look down. Strange,
there's a trail of milk across the pavement,
milk pooling in a hollow by my feet,
and I can't help it, I know I'm gonna cry.

THE RECTOR

Most Sundays he preaches of life
and death, of God in His glory,
of answers like plumb-lines
that fall from the Gospels.
His homilies carry the hues
of heaven, their glow
suffusing those in the nave
like light through stained glass.

At home in the rectory, three novels
and a volume of poetry sit side
by side with his second Bible
on an improvised shelf
above another that holds
a single clay flower pot,
its red geranium blossoms
bright as Christ's blood, the shelves
carefully fixed to fit for a while
the home-made coffin
that will stand upright
against the living-room wall
till the day he requires it.

At times when his parish
is nothing but trouble,
evenings when his golf game
is gone, his putting erratic,
he seldom passes the coffin
without a dire glance,
then a nod of his head
and a grin.

EVEN THE ATHEIST

I'm the one
crouched in the crawl space:

a clamour of footsteps hammer over my head,
voices drop through the floorboards,

noise like yapping hounds, an animal treed,
sounds that strike through the darkness

with the fangs of snakes, rubbery souls slithering,
gravel beneath my knees and hands

sharp as the barbs on number nine wire,
cold as the concrete floor of a bunker,

no heat, no trace of light from the star
affixed to the chest of my shirt. I can hear

my heart. Pounding louder and louder.
I pray God their voices cover the sound.

WHAT'S REQUIRED OF FRIENDS

We met in a gravel lot in River Park,
cars pointing east and west, drawn side by side.
You stepped from the driver's seat, your face stark,
a man lost to liquor, on a slide

toward oblivion, a twenty-two
clenched in your fist, the gun you handed me,
saying, "Here it is. I'm counting on you.
Keep it – though I fucking beg on bended knee."

I eased it through the window as you slid
back into your car, hand shaking on the wheel,
your teeth set in your lower lip like a kid
who knows he's guilty and there's no appeal.

Lord, let me forget, when your luck had run
out, how I learned you had a second gun.

A PIECE OF LUCK

He was driving the Alaska highway,
pines, and a clear sky deep as a mountain lake
when he saw something ahead in the ditch,
a brown hump swaying over long grass
where no farmer had ever mowed.
He braked once, let the car roll to a stop.
The whir of the window descending.
Over the hum of the idling engine,
he thought he heard a snuffling noise.

He turned the ignition off.
Yes, a snuffling and snorting,
another sound like the tearing of flesh.
What a piece of luck. A bear on a carcass.
He lifted the camera from the passenger seat,
eased himself from the car, slowly crossed the highway.

Where the grass was beaten down, he could see
the antlers of a dead moose, an enormous rack
that trophy hunters would die for.
That hump, he thought, it must be a grizzly,
but the angle was wrong, the animal squat and feeding.
He rose on his tiptoes, raised the camera and whistled,
the view-finder filled with rearing bear, damn, the focus
was off, the bear down and charging.

THE DRIVER

Curves through the mountains at night,
hardly a chance to pass, our headlights
raking boulders across the gorge.
On the climb, he slows till I'm down to a crawl,
but when I try to take him, he speeds up,
his Cadillac leaping ahead, rich bastard
in leather seats, laughing at me and my half-ton.
Just wait, I'll show him when to laugh.
                              No sign of lights ahead,
I get him on a corner – what's another dent
in the fender, eh? – I bump him, hit the brakes
when he slows, bump him again, force
him over. The rest in the mirror: he spins
into the ditch, bounces and rolls,
lands against a tree, his lights
shining up through the pines.
I make a slow u-turn. Wait a minute,
the guy has his door open,
stumbles up onto the road, he's
in my lights now, a dribble of blood
on his fancy jacket, I gun it toward him
– let's check his reflexes, eh? – but he doesn't
dive for the ditch, stupid bastard, when I hit him
he falls backward under the grill. I pull to a stop,
walk back toward him, flat on the pavement,
his eyes shut. He doesn't seem to be breathing,
the poor, dumb bugger. I better
roll him into the ditch,
get out of here fast.

YEARS AGO

Her memory of childhood is the burden
she carries all of her days, the priest
once more leading her into the upper room.
Each step along the way she felt hauled
through mud that meant to suck her down,
head dragged under, mouth clogged.
She gasped for air, as if shaken
from sleep, throwing off the comforter
to discover another nightmare begun.
The priest saying again, "It was your doing.
If anyone learns what happened, your parents
will have to know. That's simply how it is.
What will they think of you then?"

It was in the past, she tells herself, all of it
years ago, though sometimes it plays behind her eyes,
an erratic film in black and white, mainly black.
She yearns for comedy, spends her evenings
at the theatre, gleaning moments of respite
while all around her people rock with laughter.
When the movie ends, the house lights rise,
she tells herself that she was laughing too.

She slips into her parka, another weight
on her shoulders, and stumbles into the street,
shadows beyond every lamppost, and up ahead
a darker shadow, the cathedral, spires eclipsed by night,
the cathedral where once a child knelt in peace,
where she might kneel once more
if there was only some way to believe.

'TIS THE SEASON

Her father selects each of her presents
from under the tree, totes them outside,

drops them into the garbage bin, returns
to the front room, takes her hand, leads her

through the door. Locks it behind her.
Later her mother lets her back in the house.

Alone in the upstairs hall, she phones her friend,
is told he's out, she needn't call again.

The next day her favourite aunt draws her aside.
Doesn't she ever think of her younger cousins?

How can they live in the same town as her?
If she had any sense she'd move away.

Her father agrees she ought to leave town.
Her mother delivers her to the bus depot,

lifts a single suitcase from the trunk, deposits
it by the curb. Drives off without a word.

She wonders how she'll survive
– how they'll survive – in Vancouver.

MY OLD MAN

"Get a job," he used to say
when I was up till midnight,
red-eyed, nervous, burnt out,
cramming for first year finals.
And when I got a summer job,
plumber's helper at C & E,
"You need a better job," he said,
"something with a decent future."

But my future meant a degree.
"Anything past high school,"
he used to say, "is just an excuse
to keep sitting on your ass.
You're not getting money out of me.
Take some responsibility for once,
get out and support yourself."

At long last, my commerce degree,
and a position, accountant in a growing firm.
"A desk job," he says, "that's unbelievable.
You're still just sitting on your ass.
You'll be fat before you're forty,
then it's varicose veins and heart attacks."

Every week he calls me up, the voice
of experience with more sound advice.
"You should pick up a second job,
fix it so your wife can afford
to stay home where she belongs.
That's what every woman wants."
Yeah, my old man, who always calls collect.

COMING HOME AT NIGHT

He pulls into the driveway, snow in the headlights,
tracks smudging the walk, a drift over the shovel.
He turns off the lights, the ignition, and sits
where he is, hand gripping the wheel, radio silent,
a ping under the hood, metal contracting
as the engine cools. After a while he notes
how his hand hangs on the wheel, drops it
to the arm rest, later notices the cloud
of breath on the windshield, and beyond that
the house, no light at the front step, no light
in the windows. She must be in bed.

The streetlight down the block casts a pale glow
through the yard, and he can see curtains
closed in the master bedroom windows.
When he understands that he's shaking
with cold, he opens the car door, steps out,
picks his way through the snow and enters
the dark house. Hangs his coat in the closet,
tiptoes down the hall.

He opens the door, stands, listening,
her breathing like that of someone asleep.
He sheds his clothes in the dark, warm air
on his legs, the furnace exhaling below.
Clad only in shorts, he steps to his side of the bed,
slides under the covers, the bed sinking, a sigh
deep in the mattress. The quiet house.
He matches the pace of her breaths
with his own. How easy it is.
On the far side of the bed
her body curled like a fist.

ANOTHER DARK HOUR

When she slips from their bed in the night
he's sprawled half out of the covers, breathing
easily, right arm dangling over the mattress edge.
How can he sleep so soundly, she wonders.
She walks toward the kitchen, the hall floor
creaking as she passes the second bedroom.
The living room on the left is dark, not a hint
of light through the picture window sheers,
the street lamp on the corner burnt out again.
She stands for a while with the fridge door open,
the light falling around her as she stares
at the vegetable bin. Cold air pressing against her.
She considers the pitcher of water, reaches
for it and sets it on the counter top, the fridge door
open behind her, her slim figure framed
at the kitchen window, her image on glass.
She closes the door, looks out on the dark yard,
the ragged hedge that divides their garden
from the grounds of the school in the distance, a single light
burning in the lot where the teachers park their cars.
At this hour there are no children climbing the gym set,
no children kicking balls on the soccer field,
and she can hardly imagine them there in the light.
The pitcher forgotten on the counter before her,
she stares at the school, sombre and empty.
Her hands clasp her shoulders, but can't stop
the shivers. She turns suddenly and walks
back down the hall, the hardwood creaking
at the door of the second bedroom,
the room with the bed that is empty
and will always be empty now.

KITCHEN TALK

She talked and I listened, nothing much to say.
When she finished, I opened the dishwasher,
began to drop knives and forks into the cutlery rack
metal on metal, the clatter rising, filling the air.
I dumped out the cold coffee, set the cups
in the lower tray. Two plates
thick with congealed gravy, I rinsed:
the swirl in the sink like a flushed toilet.
I stared at the fry pan, its crust of grease,
pulled out the spatula, scraped what I could
into the garbage under the sink – globules
of fat, soggy vegetables, sinews of meat.
I shoved the pan and a pot into the washer,
closed the door hard. Done with that.

The stove-top was stained, splatters of grease,
a long triangular smear I couldn't identify.
Dish rag in the sink. I soaked it under the tap,
wrung it out and began to rub, firm,
circular motions on the stove top, pressing
hard, counter-clockwise, the circle widening,
arm beginning to tire, the smear larger now,
a fetid slough after acid rain. Behind me
I heard footsteps, like exclamation marks,
then the curt click of the closed door.

WHY THE RABBITS RUN

When you walk beyond the last house
at the end of town, beyond the graveyard,
its granite slabs sinking into the earth,
your steps are quick and lively, stride long,
legs lithe and powerful, and at the edge
of a swathed field, two feeding jackrabbits
raise their heads and stare as if attracted
by the beauty of that figure, that face that looks
neither left nor right, those eyes, fierce
and lovely, fixed on a spot straight ahead.

No rabbit can understand what it meant when,
just moments ago, standing in the kitchen,
the roast dry and shrivelled on the stove,
your husband swearing once again
there was no other woman, she was
just someone he knew from work, you wheeled
and threw, a gob of potato on the shoulder
of his suit, clatter of the pot bouncing
from wall to floor, mashed potato lumps
sliding slowly down the wall, and you
were out the door, walking fast, as you are now,
your feet striking the road like hammer blows,
your eyes never drawn to the watching rabbits,
which – as if they've seen enough to know –
turn swiftly and flee through the stubble field.

PLEASURE

She lies down with a shoe salesman,
sample cases shifted hastily from bed to chair,
light from the hotel hallway sliding under the door.

As he humps and pumps on top of her,
headboard knocking the wall above them,
she studies the ceiling over his shoulder,

the light fixture there a darker, dingier shadow
that makes her think of her husband, away again
on another prolonged business trip, she wonders

is he doing it again – right now – in some other hotel room,
and would it bother him to learn that his wife
is screwing a man whose surname she doesn't remember,

her pleasure as thin as the light squeezing under the door.
Will she tell him when he calmly returns, his brief case fat as a hog,
or will she keep it inside, save it, perhaps, for later?

The salesman finishes with a groan and a sigh, and she can't say
that this is anything like what she expected, though she feels
the pleasure will come when she lets her husband know.

UNTIL THEN IT WAS JUST LIKE ANY OTHER DAY

Slept through the alarm again, the wife
already dressed and gone to work.
Woke up and kicked the covers off,
pictured her strutting to the bus stop
in that fancy dress she paid a shitload for,
swinging that highfaluting leather purse
that's big enough to stash the moon inside.

As if she's somebody. Same as always
the coffee's bubbling on the counter,
cup and bowl and cereal set out on the table,
her dishes already washed and put away.
I pour myself a cup, add a little shot of rye,
study the ads in the morning paper –
more laughs there than on the comic page.
The whole economy in the tank, no way
I'll beat the pavement for any crap job.

I can just see her at her office computer,
more make-up on her mug than any model,
enough to cover the bruise under her eye.
Yeah, and she'll come home tonight expecting
apologies, and I'll hand them out as usual.

Oh well, time to see who's down at the Royal
and when I go to the closet for my jacket
there's nothing left of hers but old rags
– damn, she must have stuffed that purse
with everything worth taking. She's gone, sure,
but she'll be back, I know bloody well she will.

THE PARENTS' REQUEST

We would dare ask this much:
not that the farmer will run
faster when he hears the crash
and sees the roiling fountain of dust;

not that he will organize
the others more quickly, heaving
one end of the truck, forcing a rock beneath
to ease the weight, your chest rising again;

not even that you will be thrown farther,
the door wrenched wide, metal torn,
the truck rolling over and over, stopping at last
a yard from where you lie, stunned but unbroken.

No, we ask this, only this:
that before the right front wheel catches
the loose stones on the edge of the road,
before the truck launches itself at the ditch,

you will glance down at the seat belt
and snap it around your waist, the belt
that will grip you tight in the battered truck,
holding you safer than even our arms.

THE BOY'S MOTHER

I slept that night with my clothes on
though I barely slept at all. He was always
a good boy. With friends, lots of friends.
On Friday nights they filled the basement
with chips and laughter. Old movies.
Police tape around the house.
We were told to go somewhere else.
My sister's house. A bed that swayed
beneath me. I thought I'd fall on the floor.
My husband rigid as rebar beside me.
Our other son alone in the next room.
There'd be no classes tomorrow. None.

Nights later when I fell asleep
I dreamed. As I knew I would.
He was just seventeen, a boy who always
talked at breakfast, but that morning
he was out of the house, gone in the dark.
I wouldn't think of the other parents.
Making arrangements. Should we
just throw him into the ground?
Didn't we need to say goodbye?

We had no idea, how could we,
did we do something wrong?
He planned it – how could anyone know?
– with another boy, just the two of them.
The school where he went with his friends.
Tired and I can't stay awake, the dream
again, and again, the boy with the gun,
our son, the hole in his head, bleeding,
our son dead, and he keeps on shooting.

ANOTHER MORNING AFTER

His mind burning with the idea
he can't quite grasp – something
he stalked moments ago
in a dream, a cougar padding silently
through shadows, but gone into the woods
each time he raised his rifle, or was he
the beast fleeing a man with a gun?

He steps out of the shabby bedroom,
rumpled pants draped on the chair behind him,
socks and shorts by his shoes on the floor,
empty bottle of scotch beside them.
Yawning, rubbing the bruise on his hip,
he walks through the rented house,
his eyes closing each time he yawns.
He stands naked in the open veranda,
shivering, his bad knee beginning to ache.

In the east the sky is already bright,
a line above the dark hills as red,
he knows, as the whites of his eyes.
Another morning on its way, one day
after another till it's over, and never
a sign that anything matters at all.
His mouth dry as the fluff under the bed,
he stares and stares at the morning sky,
astounded once more he's glad to be here.

Currents, roiling

A DARK CURRENT FLOWING

I slid down a mountain of shale to the library
where they planned to give away signed copies
and was stopped by a tiny, pink-faced man
who complained of fallen arches and sore heels.
Not to worry, they wouldn't be fatal, I told him
and asked how well his heart was pumping.
Before he could answer, I found myself
on the river bank, an unpainted clapboard shack
the size of a triple garage, not a door in sight,
but I stood inside, sunlight falling through broken boards
and on my father, fresh from the grave, strapping
canvas tarpaulins over a motor boat
he had never owned, a tangle of bungee cords
like a nest of snakes at his feet, one hissing,
its tail wrapped around a silver pan
the size of a colander that he picked up
and set on the workbench, but it slid off,
bounced, and spun toward him, the workbench
made of ice and beginning to melt, my father
staring down at the spinning pan, which I grabbed
before it whirled me six times around, but I got it
back on the bench though the bench was a wave
that tossed it aside, a wave that surged forward
and picked up the boat, heaved it against a beam
that splintered and fell, the boat collapsing,
broken and flattened beneath it. Useless.
My father shook his head which rose
through a hole in the roof, shook it,
and said in the dry voice of a stranger:

"If it's any consolation, we can't always
be blamed for what happens around us."
He studied me a moment, nodded then,
mounted a pair of stilts and slowly skated away.

DORMEZ-VOUS

Evening arrives like a cattle truck
bumping slow down an old dirt road,
wind-blown dust rolling before it.
It's not my job to unload the steers.
I gaze at the stars, pale in the hazy sky,
the moon an ice cube for the palm of my hand.
Smell of manure sifts through the air,
cattle bawling in a feedlot nearby.
The taste of raw meat on my tongue again,
a taste that cuts like a knife through the palate,

the Swiss Army knife of Luke Cody who sliced
my index finger in the vacant lot behind his house
the day we swore we'd be blood brothers forever.
Oh man, we could barely believe in tomorrow.
His grandparents sat on their back porch bench,
Life magazines open on both of their laps,
but all they seemed to be reading was us.
Frayed gotch hung in a row on the porch rail;
they were out of clothes pins and the porch creaked.
Mosquitoes are a drag – bad as hot flashes,
the old lady said, slapping her husband's cheek.

The chill shiver of evening shakes me
out of that day that wasn't forever.
I feel almost as warm as burnt toast
after a cold night in the garbage.
No wonder I try to fire up the barbecue,
but it sparks and sparks, refusing to light.
Luke the Puke would've known what to do,
but I haven't seen him since August, 1973,

though tomorrow – or some other tomorrow –
he'll climb up the trellis again
and tap on my bedroom window,
the atomic touch of his index finger
blasting me out of my bed,
knocking the sleep from my eyes.
I'll know it's Luke as soon as he leaves.

Frère Luka, Frère Luka,
dormez-vous, dormez-vous?
our grade nine song repeats in my head
and the evening slides out from behind
the wheel of the truck, pulls on a pair
of Tumalo hiking boots, laces them up,
and strides into the dark and infinite night.

FREE BREAKFAST AT THE COMFORT INN

The room crowded, tables small, my parents at one,
my older brother and I at another, I saw the woman

at the next table slide the scarlet nail of her index finger
under the skin of the mandarin and begin to strip

the peel away from the lush orange pulp below.
My brother, the teenager, glanced at our parents

and stopped eating his muffin, which, without looking,
he set on his styrofoam plate, his eyes on the woman

with the scarlet fingernails, that one nail moving
steadily under the skin of the orange which fell

away, revealing more bright flesh,
the orange cupped, round and fresh, in her palm.

She tore off one section, her nail
piercing the flesh, a sudden spurt of juice,

and she took that piece of orange on her tongue
and drew it slowly into her mouth, my brother

sliding the paper napkin from the table
and dropping it onto the lap of his jeans.

I was young then, watching my brother,
and wondered why I was blushing.

UNDER THE PILLOW

Velma Jean shivered all the way up the hill,
the log cabin hidden in the trees of Cobweb Bluff.
She wasn't sure she could face Auntie Womack
with her question; Auntie Womack was no aunt of hers,
nor of anyone here in Bucksnort Hollow; an odd creature,
she knew the things that no one else knew.

The old woman had told her father the trick
for relieving his frequent attacks of gout,
herbs gathered by a full moon at midnight
but only ingested in the heat of high noon.
Velma Jean hesitated on the stone walk,
the image of Clyde Duckett firm in her mind.

She could do it, yes, of course, she'd do it for him.
She stepped forward and knocked. Waited
on tiptoes, ready to flee. The door creaked open,
an old woman with a gnarled hand on the knob,
sparse grey hair falling from a green bandana,
a livid red scar across the cords of her throat,

but eyes that twinkled above furrowed cheeks.
This might be possible. Clyde Duckett,
she said, was the fellow she wanted to marry.
Auntie Womack warned her to be in bed by ten,
every night for a week, a mirror under her pillow.
On the fifth night Clyde Duckett entered her dreams,

Clyde with a line of children behind him, five gawky girls
and four little boys, two of them toddlers, the last two in diapers.
Velma Jean woke with a start, her head throbbing.
She groped beneath her pillow, found the mirror
and smashed it against the wall. Clyde Duckett
need never know why she'd snub him the rest of her days.

PEOPLE STILL CALL IT THE BECKETT PLACE

The fourth house from the corner
of Cop Shop Road and Second Avenue
is the one the neighbours say is haunted.
Some nights at midnight, long after the Sawyers
have put out their lights and gone to bed,
you'll see a dim glow in the third floor window,
a shadow moving slowly across the curtain.
If you didn't know better you might think
when it paused it was looking down
at the For Sale sign on the front lawn.

Sometimes, when the Sawyers are out,
you can hear sounds from behind the window,
a broken scream, then a low moaning
that soon gives way to repeated sobs.
On Christmas Eve when the Sawyers always
leave home to be with their out-of-town daughter,
the window frame on the third floor
will shake and rattle till you wonder
what keeps the glass from cracking.
People say it's been this way for thirty-two years
– since that dark and starless Christmas Eve when
Old Man Beckett found his young second wife
in bed with his widowed son-in-law
and beat them bloody with a candlestick.

That night the window frame shook and bucked,
the noise so loud it startled a cop on foot patrol.
He knocked and knocked without an answer,
the rattling and rapping unabated above him.
Finally, with the aid of the town locksmith,
he made his way inside, forced himself
to mount the dark stairs to the third floor.

No light switches here, it seemed,
but in the beam of his flashlight
he found, hanging from the rafters,
the lean body of Old Man Beckett,
his boots a few inches above the floor
turning and turning in a clockwise direction.
Not another soul could be found in the house
except the locksmith quaking by the front door
and the two bodies sprawled on a third-floor bed.

THIS TIME OF NIGHT

If I had half a brain, I'd rush to the window,
lean far over the street, and hurl epithets
at the man below, who almost every night,
after the bars close, halts his wavering homeward walk
to piss on my ornamental fence, his stream
like that of an elephant, splashing through the pickets
to drench my marigolds, a ricocheting yellow spray
– on his socks for all I know, the man leaning
back on his heels with his hips thrust forward,
his shadow beneath like a humpbacked dwarf.

I imagine myself climbing up to the sill,
carefully bracing my feet, and taking a leak on him,
soaking him through and through, until, steeped
in urine, he collapses, like corrugated cardboard
saturated, and he's washed into the gutter. Then
wrap him in plastic, toss him through the open door
of a boxcar, railroad him right out of town,
forever off my street. Instead I sacrifice
my marigolds, hold my piss and my voice.
Maybe tomorrow – tomorrow night I'll get the guy.

THE WAY IT HAPPENS

Slow-dancing at sock hops in the gym,
long afternoons at the beach, the night
at the drive-in his hand fell on her breast
and she hardly dared breathe, afraid
he'd move it away, this boy that she loved.

Then his father was transferred east,
his parents insisting he go with them.
She begged him to stay and finish grade twelve,
but he went with the family. Left her behind.
Empty as the pant leg of an amputee.

Forty years on, married, half a continent away,
she heard the news of the crash that killed him.
Too bad, she said, nodding, then shaking her head.
Fifteen years later an old friend mentions his name
and she isn't quite sure: Is he alive or dead?

SIGNS OF HEALING

For Ken

Flesh peeled back from his jaw, bone
removed, replaced with a shard from his leg,
stitches concealed in the lines of his face,
the cancer engaged by radiation, and chemo,
then a screw coming loose, infection, another
procedure, a metal plate this time, daily trips
to Home Care for a change of dressings,
today he welcomes visitors, offers them drinks
though there can be no alcohol for him.

His face swathed in bandages, a tube
beneath to drain excess fluids, two dogs
curled at his feet, their coats white
as his dressing. His mouth hurts,
he admits, but he drinks Boost, manages
some meat if it's cut small enough.

His wife has taken to feeding stray cats
at the back door, worries about what they'll drink
when the temperature plummets. He considers.
"I could add anti-freeze to their water," he says.
"Oh no, it's poison," she says, "it would kill them."
"Gee, I never thought of that." A mischievous grin,
we know, hidden beneath the bandages.

NOVEMBER 16TH

For Donna

She's reading microfilm when I enter the archives.
Today, she tells me, would be her parents' 68th anniversary.
The archives – temperature controlled, the room always cold.
No, she says, November's not a strange month for a wedding,
her parents were farmers, too busy too much of the time.
No pictures on the dull grey walls around us here.
Yes, they're both gone now, her mother
eight years ago, her father thirty-seven.
Heart attacks – both of them – gone like that!

When her father died, she didn't see
how she could get through the day
but, of course, she did. She had to.
No doubt a heart attack is how she'll go too.
A good way for her, she says, swift
and efficient, not so good for those left behind.
She turns back to her reading, the hum
of the microfilm reader like the buzz
of bees on the farm, a warm June morning,
her mother's flowers just beginning to bloom.

WHAT HIS MOTHER SAID

"Sometimes," she said, "a man's flaws
are the size of elephants.
They might be rearing, trumpeting,
but he wouldn't notice a thing."
The boy was sure she meant his father,
was just as sure she wouldn't say it.
"I think I understand you," she said,
"but who knows by the time you're grown?
Most men are a mystery to their wives,
themselves too. They don't say what they mean.
Fact is, they seldom know it themselves."

The end of the day as long as the sun,
a pale moon already riding the sky,
the boy with his nose at the window
watching his father trudge in from the field,
his hand slapping bugs on the back of his neck.
His mother began to slice the overdone roast,
a cross-rib, he supposed, his father's favourite.
"Wealth," he remembers her telling him once,
"isn't the money you store in the bank."
The sound of the opening door. The blaze
that flared in her eyes like the candle flame
when she let him light the wick at Easter.

WHAT HE LOVES

His wife longs for a home in the city,
her mother there already, wanting
frequent visits in the nursing home,
their daughter too, and the little girls.

He thinks of the line of trees at the farm,
the story of wind they tell at dawn,
the first light painting again a brilliant sky.
There's farm work to do, he won't retire.
No, he'll have to commute to his own land.

His wife finds a house she likes, open
spaces and plenty of room – it'll do, he supposes.
They make an offer, raise it once,
and sign the deal. Begin moving furniture,
the home on the farm growing hollow, forlorn.
A hole in his chest and no way to fill it.

Their house in the city, not a tree,
not a bush on this scrap of land, a front lawn
you could spit across. He thinks of the farm,
grass sweeping out to the road, the porch
where he watches the sun sink in a sea of red.
He loves his wife, he knows he does, but the view
from here is the doors of a double garage.

RETIRED FARMER

His is the only house on the street
with action in the kitchen this early, coffee burbling,
bacon sizzling, spattering the stove top.
In the old days he'd have been in the field
an hour by now. He eats slowly, taking
small bites of his toasted bacon sandwich,
washing each down with a swallow of coffee.
Another long day ahead. He listens
to the Ag Report on the radio, wishes
Ellen were here to discuss it with him;
they could argue the benefits of seeding canola.
When he's done eating, he steps to the sink,
slowly washes and dries his dishes, stacks them
one by one back in the cupboard.
He selects a cap from the shelf by the door,
the Co-op logo stained with sweat.
A working man's cap, he thinks, it fits
like his goatskin welding gloves once fit,
and who knows where they are today?

He steps outside, sun already up in the east.
His square of lawn is not overgrown, but he opens
the shed doors, gazes at his John Deere riding mower,
model D105, 17.5 horsepower, 42 inch cutting system.
He mounts the seat, starts the engine,
drives out of the shed, engine growling,
much smoother than his old Massey-Harris tractor
that squawked like a bull calf on castration day.
Angry faces glare from neighbours' windows.

Well, it's time they were up anyway. Besides,
they probably think he looks foolish
riding this patch of lawn, but the steering wheel
throbs in his hand and there's work to be done.
He turns a corner and turns again, taking it
slow, overlapping each cut by an inch or two,
until at last he circles, in the centre of the lawn
a flower bed about the size of a grave.
When the grass is cut, he'll hose down the deck
of the cutting system, flush out the grass buildup.
Then he'll think about the rest of the day,
and tomorrow, and the days after that.

ON THE NOLAND FARM

Near Junction City, Kansas, November, 1911

John Noland is sick to death of the rock pile
he must work around every time he seeds his wheat.
Today he loads boulder after boulder on the stoneboat,
concludes this isn't natural, someone must've put them here.
If you didn't know better you'd take it for the mark
of a crazy man. Every rock removed at last, he scrapes
away a mound of dirt – more damned rock.
Great unhewn stones lie together. Almost
like a wall. Must be nearly ten feet thick.
He digs some more, knows he'll miss his supper,
keeps on digging, scoops soil from within the wall,
and under the soil, more stones, you'd think
a roof had fallen in; yeah, probably crushed
by the weight of earth upon it. A roof or an arch.
Good Lord, could this be some kind of tomb?
He removes more stones. No. Only earth beneath.

He steps closer to the wall, digs there,
the twilight coming on. His shovel strikes
another rock. He works beneath it, stoops
to roll it free, but this one is long. He levers it up,
one end rising; he lifts and pulls, discovers
he's holding what appears to be a thigh bone,
much longer, thicker than any human femur.
There were Indians here, he thinks, for centuries,
but he's never heard of giants. He shakes his head
and wonders. Decides to dig some more.
In moments he unearths a skull, a human skull,
much larger than his own, above one eye
a gaping hole where once a weapon struck.
The skull in his hands, he lifts his head
and gazes at the sky, darkness gathering,
a star in the east pulsing like a warning.

ABSENT

Conrad wasn't at school that day.
We were all of us bent over our scribblers,
writing letters precisely between the lines,
trying for swooping loops on the "e"s and "l"s,
doing it right, just like Miss Brevick, her white
letters marching in rows over the blackboard.
If Conrad was scrunched here in the desk beside me,
he'd write every letter once, a single line
smooth and unbroken, a twenty-six letter word
we'd never pronounce, and then he'd draw.

No stick-men for Conrad, I liked to watch
from the side of my eye, a real boy spinning
out of his pen, a boy running or climbing a tree,
sometimes a man with a big stick, and the sky
– he was always drawing the sky – clouds swelling
and swirling, cyclones and lightning, hail in the wind.
After school I played tag until supper-time,
but it wasn't much fun without Conrad.

That night when we sat down to eat,
my father switched off the news,
my mother looking at me and him.
After supper he ripped out the funny page,
tore it right out of the *Times*, gave it to me,
and went off with the rest of the paper.
At bedtime, they read to me, both of them read,
a chapter each from *Winnie the Pooh*.

The next morning I couldn't wait for the bell.
I ran into the school, right up to Miss Brevick
and asked her when Conrad was coming back.
Her mouth fell open, a round and perfect
"O," but not a sound came out of that "O."
I started to cry, and so did Miss Brevick,
her shoulders beginning to shake, her arms
reaching for me, and I didn't know why.

AFTER MY SISTER MARRIES FOR THE FOURTH TIME

At the reception my father gazes at his new shoes
ablaze in the light from the raised window,
gazes and sighs, black leather shining
like a mirror that holds an image:
his walker shoved against the couch
where he can always reach it. He sags,
spine like a worn spring, his head
tipped onto his chest.

I pass him food, carrot sticks
and egg salad sandwiches,
the buns soggy with mayonnaise.
He takes a single carrot stick, plays
with it, rolls it between his fingers,
raises it toward his lips, pauses,
lays it at last back on the plate.

When night finally falls,
it's the upstairs room of the old house,
black shingles pulsing for days
in summer sunshine, summer heat.
I lie again on the old bed and listen,
my father in the room below,
the squealing wheel of his walker
that says again how he feels.

ON THE FRONT LAWN

We thought them a handsome pair indeed,
the young couple who moved in next door.
When he introduced his wife, his words
shone with the pride of winning a woman
so lovely, her complexion like ivory, hair dark
as the night of a single star. On evenings in June
when windows were open, we'd hear radio music
and sometimes detect two voices singing along.

Once, just before dark, their western windows
stained with the red of a sinking sun,
she ran from the house and hurled herself
onto the front lawn, beating her fists in the grass.
He knelt beside her, bending close to her ear,
whispering, stroking her hair until she rose
and, his arm around her waist, he helped her inside.

The next month it happened again. And the next.
Again a week later. And the very next day,
the young husband standing on his front step,
slowly shaking his head, frightened,
perhaps, or cringing, who could tell,
while his wife lay on the lawn, pounding
and tearing the grass, moaning,
her words incoherent, a gibber
no neighbour would ever decipher.
And what about him? we wondered.
How much did he understand?

Darkness, gathering

ON THE VALUE OF RESEARCH

Two grad students and their English professor
come to town to question our writing group,
research for papers they'll write some day.
Three good hours of talk, then a tour of the town.
They'd like to see the trestle that reaches
through so many stories and poems. We drive
to South Hill, park off the road in the weeds,
walk back to the trestle, that focus
of nightmare and dream, black skeletal
girders sweeping over the river, the tracks
and ties above, a dark network of ribs.

I tell them about a scene in a story, two boys
on that girder, one of them wanting to jump,
a scene that refuses to work,
                                                            until one fall night
I try some practical research, climb onto the girder,
rivets like ice cubes striking my knees, black paint
flaking from metal, white splatters of pigeon shit,
hum of distant trucks on the highway, a throbbing
pump here on the river bank, stagnant water
and a swampy smell – getting the details right,
and praying no student of mine will happen along
and catch his teacher perched on a trestle.

I say not a word about what it was like
as a child – following the bigger boys, caught
out on that girder, the river below and me unable
to swim, both hands clutching metal, afraid
to crawl ahead because I'd have to let go
with one hand and I knew that I'd fall – and let them
try it themselves, I think, then they'll know.

CLASSMATES

Sometimes I still think of you, Peter Kooy,
though it's over half a century since we were
pharmacy classmates together, the two of us
meeting at times in the cold of winter
on the 25th Street Bridge as we hurried
back to the U of S gym for an evening
of intramural basketball, me trying to match
your long strides, just as later I'd try
to go as high as you on my layups.
You a teammate always willing
to pass off the ball, a lab partner
eager to share your latest discovery.
Our last party at graduation, fuelled
in part by lab alcohol, and we ended
up in your basement suite, more drunk
on dreams than alcohol, and that night
was the last time I ever saw you
though in '77 I passed through Lethbridge
and gave you a call, your friendly voice
still recognizable after a decade and a half,
both of us parents now, but eager to talk of old times,
and back again in '97, no sign of your name
in the phone book, a series of calls
to one drugstore after another – were these
youngsters on the line? – none of them
knew a Peter Kooy, the name meant nothing
to them, a sudden surge of sorrow then, and later
I'd learn what I already knew must be true.

PALACE FRUIT

On Main Street at Palace Fruit we bought
the sunflower seeds we couldn't buy
in the Royal Theatre, a frenzy of chewing
through Saturday afternoon serials, shells
sprayed on the floor, Batman chained
to the tracks, a locomotive roaring
toward the trestle. Throats constricted, mouths
dry from the impact, we'd rush to Palace Fruit
for a Coke, Fred, the owner, cracking
caps off glistening bottles from his antique cooler.

The store was long and narrow, a lunch counter
running from the front till to a room in the back,
the place so narrow you had to step sideways
to get to a stool. Was it a store or a cafe he ran?
You could buy bananas in bunches, apples, oranges,
and we never saw anyone eat a meal at his counter
though some with stomachs of steel dared his hot dogs.
We wondered if Fred slept in the back room.

In high school, after a night of shooting pool
– smoke drifting over green felt, always
a butt in our mouths like the old hockey stars
who played for money on the front table –
we'd stop for a treat on the way home.
Fred's apple pie from a mass-market bakery
was cheap, and a la mode it cleared the stale
taste of smoke from our mouths.

Years later, married and settled, home
for a reunion, we walk the changed streets
of our old town, and passing Palace Fruit, we pause
at its hazy front window, cobwebs and a tattered blind,
the store empty – except at the darkened doorway in back,
a gaunt figure hovers, a lean phantom in a white apron.

609 MAIN SOUTH

The meals in a black bag packed in styrofoam,
you cart them out to the car, place the meals-on-wheels card
on the dash, check the delivery list, and there it is,
the address you'll never forget, your family home,
where you lived from grade three to grade twelve
and the year you worked saving money for college.
You deliver the other meals, keep this one for last.

From the car, you see a garage in the backyard
where Nipper's doghouse stood, the lawn
where you staggered walking tall
on homemade wooden stilts, vinyl siding
covering the stucco you helped your father paint.
You climb the steps where you posed in your first suit
the day you graduated from high school.
You ring the buzzer at the front doorway
you haven't entered in thirty-one years.

A Chinese man opens the door, ushers you in.
Shuffling backwards, he motions to a small table
in the entryway. "Just put it here," he says.
Hands shaking, you extract his main course,
his soup and dessert, place them on the table.
"When I was a kid," you say, "I used to live here."
His eyes are on his meal, but he nods, says,
"Uh huh. Been here fourteen years myself."

You lean into the living room, bare hardwood,
not an area rug in sight, nor the sofa on whose back
you rested your elbows gazing out the window,
watching the snow fall and cover the street
where you and your friends played road hockey.
All the old furniture is gone, of course,
as are your parents, an abyss opening
inside, and you realize, oh Lord,
how much you still miss them.

THE TOWN HE REMEMBERS

He pulls off the Yellowhead, finds Railway Avenue in Paynton,
no sign of McGee's General Store where the clerks knew his name,
no sign of Joe Luke's Cafe where Joe sliced him free cherry pie.
He swings the truck and trailer to the side of the street,
stares at the road running south. Little chance for a u-turn there.
"My grandmother's house," he says, "is up this way."
His wife and kids follow him out of the truck,
along a line of pines and broken poplars
toward the last house at the end of town.

Two storeys, weathered clapboard, empty windows.
The hobby horse that he rode will be gone now,
and the Indian hammer from Cut Knife Creek.
Yes, and the wind-up bird he feared
with the beak that might seize his ear.
No trace of the barn with the deer's head on the wall,
the dark eyes that stared and stared at his own.
He points to an upstairs window.
"I remember watching a storm from there,
the whole house starting to shake
black clouds rolling in, not even noon,
the town and prairie dark as night."

The kids keep glancing back at the truck,
edging away. There's not much to see.
A screen door opens across the road,
a woman steps out, hands on her hips.
We aren't trespassing, he thinks,
but she's calling them over. He explains
about Grandma Mondy, but she shakes her head,

says they were looking at Gus Schrank's place,
Ida Mondy's house was the next one south,
torn down years ago to make for a bigger field
when the price of wheat was high. He feels
disoriented, a bit foolish, but she invites them in,
offers them lemonade and cookies, asks
about his mom, his aunts, and he thinks
it's still the town he remembers.

AUNT MYRTLE

Pink and charcoal was the newest craze
and Aunt Myrtle was going to buy me a shirt,
but when she motioned for the salesclerk,
I heard her say, "That one, girlie, the one right there."
I wanted to run away, oh man, but I wanted to try it on,
I prayed she wouldn't use that word again.
The clerk carrying the shirt, her back straight
as a two-by-four, her face in a smile
stiff and phony as a mannequin's chest.
Aunt Myrtle said, "This is the latest thing,
ain't it, girlie?" the woman nodding her head,
not a single word. I loved my Aunt Myrtle,
but I would have given anything to be anywhere else.

Walking out of the store, parcel under my arm,
my cheeks burning for the salesclerk,
I tried to focus on a story my mother once told,
a hard time years before I was born,
her older sister Myrtle on a dead-end farm
out by Little Pine Reserve, someone's deserted homestead,
she and her first husband not quite making a go of it,
but hanging on through a bad winter, walls white with frost,
a long dark night in January. Knocking on the door.

The light from her kerosene lantern fell
on a Cree family, two small children
with blankets clutched around them, a man
and woman, clothing made of animal pelts
that hung like skin loose on their bones, Aunt Myrtle

inviting them in, settling them at the table
while she added a few more scraps of meat
to the thin stew already gurgling on the stove.
The government, she'd said, damned government,
they would have let those poor people starve.

WATCHER IN THE RAIN

The rain falls on the grass, the grain beyond the graves,
the single open grave, the windshield through which she watches
the casket where her sister's body will remain,
pools of rain forming on the casket lid, rivulets
running down its gentle curve, falling in the pit.

Her younger sister. She remembers the two of them
dancing at the end of an Oklahoma drought, the rain
like a drum beating, beating on the roof as they jigged
past Father pitching hay in Bessie's stall,
spinning in the rain, heads thrown back,
mouths open, half-insane with laughter, collapsing
in the mud, and Father, who might complain,
only smiled at them, Father at the barn door,
hat in his hand, dark hair shining in the rain.

Her sister barely eighty-eight, and oh the pain,
the grief, how could she be the first to go?
Her little sister whom she loved to dress
in pinafores and show off in town on Saturdays,
the two of them driven once from the boardwalk
into Owen's General Store by a cloudburst.
Her friend invited them above the store
to play in the storage room, but they stood
on empty crates that might have made a playhouse,
and leaned against a fractured window pane,
a team of horses at the hitching post below,
heads lowered, manes drenched, raindrops
bouncing from their shaggy backs, splashing
in the stream that soon ran above their hooves.

The girls craned their necks and saw
beyond the town the plain become a lake,
the rain a river down the pane on which
their noses pressed,
                                        no wipers beating there like these
that fling the rain away and seem to say again,
"She's dead, she's dead, your little sister's dead."
That one refrain as bleak and steady as the rain.

READING THE PAPER

Turning in haste from the sports page,
"Roughriders Hammered in Hamilton,"
I see your photo, Gord, gazing at me
exactly as you did the last time we met,
that trace of a smile, a cordial hello,
the conversation dying soon after
– I guess we haven't met in half a dozen years –
and I remember too your first wife, Maxine, dead
now for what must be a decade and a half,
a South Hill girl, someone I admired,
and her brothers, slick athletes who could
gobble ground balls like Yankee shortstops.
Bobby, I recall, on the King Edward team with me,
the school itself demolished years ago, rubble
for the city landfill, the arch from the main door
relocated to Crescent Park, just another relic,
but I can still picture Bobby charging to his right,
diving through the school hedge to nab a foul ball,
something I might have done myself then, and now
I bend over the newspaper, the obit of a man
who, like me, has long drawn a pension,
the print blurring an instant as I read
about someone I hardly knew.

UP HERE

We are better off if we can just
climb the stairs instead of descending

at noon to the parking lot, car after car
aimed at the exit, people wanting out,

right now, before the clock spins time away.
Up the stairs, seven flights to the roof,

we bend through a low door into sunshine.
Sky like a blue promise of pleasure,

the city below in straight lines and squares,
people rushing off for something to buy.

We stroll to the wall, climb onto the parapet,
and sit, feet dangling over the cornice, the air

in our lungs as fresh as a Ted Kooser poem,
up here where the pigeons circle

around us, impatient as men
in a band with rented instruments,

the auditorium locked, no place to play,
but we are here, lunch bags open beside us,

our chatting a kind of play, our feet
swinging to a lazy rhythm, the moments

moving together and on, the noon hour
passing away too soon.

A RARE AFTERNOON

October third, here in Saskatchewan, a day
often closer to winter snow than summer heat,
all the long afternoon we sit on lawn chairs
near the crest of a hill overlooking the lake,
water still as slate, except where gulls paddle,
aimlessly, small ripples ebbing behind them.
Bare arms and legs immersed in sunlight,
we read and doze, or study the brown hills
across the lake, bare trees lining ravines,
rows of soldiers stripped of camouflage.
At times we gaze at a point of land,
its sliver of beach, a lone fisherman casting
a silver spoon, its sudden spangle of light
on still water. We doze and read, pausing now
and then to sip ice water from the thermos,
to listen to a crow caw in the valley behind.

When the light begins to change and the hills grow
melancholy, when the mosquitoes arrive,
we pack up, drive home, stubble
by the road where the haying is done,
a red glow on the horizon, dust
hanging over a distant field, a truck
in the haze, combine churning toward it.
Home with the dusk, we regard the lawn,
a jumble of leaves brought down
by September's wind and frost, the bodies
of pears that never ripen, yellow and brown,
lurid in the half-light, rotting on the grass.
A perfect afternoon over, we shrug,
then walk to the shed for shovel and rake.

THE MOST BEAUTIFUL THING IN THE WORLD

A dozen cars at the light and he knows
it's going to be red again before he gets through.
He squeezes into the right lane, turns
on the red light, makes a left at the next corner
– man, he doesn't have time for this –
but he's moving again in the right direction.
Sure, and he needs to be there a minute ago.
Some old guy in front of him, a bit younger
than him, maybe, but driving like a turtle,
afraid to jam his foot on the gas, the jerk.
Gun it around him and down the street,
then left on the next block, pull into the driveway.
Maybe he can make it yet. Out of the car,
both knees stiff as he hauls himself upright.
Get them moving, they'll come around.
Damned doorknob, key never works the first time.
Jam it in hard, crank it to the right, doorknob
pops, swing the door open, he's here at last.
No time to take off his shoes. Down the hall,
through the door on his left, and there it is,
elegant as art straight from the kiln,
lucent white curves, trim ceramic lines.
He gropes at his fly, one brief gush,
then he dribbles into the bowl, this time
only a single drop on his pants.

WALKING THE WIRE

for Flash

In my mind I sometimes walk the high wire.
The circus may have long ago moved on,
and I may be watching a November football game,
shivering, lower body stuffed into a sleeping bag,
but I'll stare at the wire behind the scoreboard.

And it's no lie to say the evening
sun will burn the sinking clouds
until the western sky is full of fire,
but still the lights of Taylor Field
will shine, bright as the floodlights

in any tent the Shriners ever owned.
The man with season tickets next to mine
has a voice even louder than yours, Flash,
and his hands will slap my hands
every time the Riders score.

So I should be content to watch
from my seat beside him, both of us
wearing Rider caps, green and white, colours
as common here as peanut shells in the aisle,
but instead I long for the wire that vanishes

into the charred and distant dark, the sun gone
as surely as the cheers we heard when we ran out
together, charging onto the high school football field,
knowing both of us that day had made the team.
No way to walk the wire to then, or even back to you.

THE LAST READING

She remembers when first they asked her
to give the reading at church her hands shook.
The thought of standing before the congregation,
all those people in the pews, everyone staring at her.
How would she ever manage it?
Her legs would quake, her voice falter,
she'd probably drop the Bible on the floor.

"You can do it," Joe said. "We'll practice at home."
Her good husband getting her to stand and read
while he sat before her, a congregation of one,
telling her she was doing fine, but she could
slow it down here, raise her voice there for effect.
She read the passage from Genesis again and again.
Read it at last in church, scripture flowing through her
like the Jordan River sweeping off to the sea.
After that, whenever she was asked to read,
she rehearsed with Joe, her confidence growing.

Today she fears her voice will waver,
but she'll do the reading anyway, will do it
for Joe, who's with her here in church.
She steadies herself, takes a deep breath,
catches the scent of fresh roses,
the pastel arrangement on the coffin lid.
A deep breath, and she does it for him.

REMEMBRANCE DAY

The camera pans across the faces, old men
who stare straight ahead and wait,
their jaws clenched and raised, their legs
braced as if the cold wind might topple them.
Their cheeks are wrinkled, marked
by blemishes that come with age,
but they seem neither weary nor weak.
Many wear glasses now and squint into the wind
that hurls itself across the hill and whips
pant legs around their thinning calves.
The wind is nothing. They've seen worse.
Felt worse. The expressions on their faces
seem to say they see again what they saw once,
their gaze in the grip of distant lands, distant times.
These faces turn neither left nor right, grim icons
of an inner strength, sculpted
by the past. After the silence,
only then, as the first wreath is laid,
do they focus on the cenotaph.
When the guns fire here, it's a martial salute.
Elsewhere in the world war is raging now
as it did then. They know and understand.

ON THE BEACH AT NIGHT

Beneath our bare feet the sand is cold,
the sky above black as a root cellar's pit.

From somewhere comes a light, dull and blear,
suffusing the line where water slaps the shore.

It may be foolish walking this strange beach at night.
When we stop to listen, we look around,

detect footprints aimed at where we stand.
The night is vast and silent here

though we catch the pulse of a failing heart,
sounds easy to explain: the wind died an hour ago,

water moving still, waves lapping at the land.
Beyond us as we turn to stare, the trees are shadows

dim and indistinct as last night's fading dream;
behind the trees dark hills disappear into the sky.

Ahead of us, where it seems a point of land
merges with the lake, the shadows are denser still.

Smaller than the night, we find each other's hands
are cold, and walk forward – propelled toward the dark.

BEFORE AND AGAIN

The car always starts like a dream,
motor catching at once, not quite a purr,
the sound of a cat crouched by a bowl of milk,
a robin beside it, feathers bloodied and torn.
I check the rear view mirrors, left side and right,
slip the gear shift into reverse, back slowly
down the driveway, the house across the street
lurching a yard or more out of the way,
the car picking up speed, weaving slightly
as I turn it onto the street. I shove at the shift,
but it won't slide into Drive – blasted car
will only go backwards. I swivel my head
side to side, and there are cars coming
behind me, three squealing by on the left,
a truck squeezing between me and the curb,
not enough room, side mirror clipped and gone.
My breath caught in my chest, I can hardly
hold the damned wheel, sweat on my palms,
I'm cinched in by the seat belt, the car
taking off now, faster and faster, I have to
stop it, a siren blaring, houses jerking by, people
in windows pointing, the car hitting a bump and bouncing,
airborne an instant, and faster still, I fight to get my foot
on the brake, body slick with sweat,
my ankle straining and caught, the tangled
sheet tight on my leg. It's happened
before. I know it'll happen again.

ACCIDENTS

After the collision in the parking lot
– I'm sure it wasn't my fault,
her car backing out just as I entered the lane,
its bumper caught on the hub of my back wheel –
I think of my father claiming he wasn't old
at 84,
            cataracts clouding his right eye,
one minor collision after another,
till he strayed to the edge of a country road,
loose gravel grabbing the wheel, the car
rolled over, battered, tossed at the ditch,
he and my mother pinned in their seat belts,
just a few bruises, but the car a write-off.

Another one purchased within a week.

Pleas then to stop driving, desperate
phone calls to the authorities, an appalling
wait until they lifted his license at last,
the stricken look on my mother's face,
no, she said, they can't do that to us,
we need to get out and around.

                                                That torn
bumper lying in the Safeway lot, and I
swear it wasn't my fault. It's not
starting with me.

THE PROCEDURE

After months of waiting for the appointment,
a half hour before your spinal procedure,
the anesthetist says if you were his grandpa
he'd cancel the surgery, too risky, maybe try again
in four months – after they've dealt with your heart.
They keep you in the hospital, give you
an angiogram, find there's a faulty valve to replace.
They open you up and discover heart muscle
in worse shape than anyone imagined.
Hours in the O.R., a difficult surgery completed,
but, Lorne, your heart isn't ready to kick in.
Joy, your wife, gives us the news, no spinal procedure
and now this, prognosis dismal, but they'll keep you
on the heart-lung machine, wait twelve hours,
and see what happens.

Our minds stumble around
like drunks lost in the dark,
just too much to take in.
We turn instead to the old days:
trips to San Francisco when we were young,
that joyous night with the Dillards at the Hungry I,
singing along with banjo bands in North Beach,
a side-trip to Salinas and Steinbeck's Cannery Row,
the stop-over in Reno, the drunken motel clerk
who kept giving us coupons for free nickels
in the casinos, Joy, Gwen and I winning
till the slots paid for our motel, you insisting
we go back the next morning and you'd
get your jackpot too. Which you did.

Crater Lake on the way home, a blue
as deep as heaven, and the cabin
we shared, four bucks per couple per night,
a box of free pine cones at the door.

We want to think of the good times,
but it's hard, hard; we sit down and soon
there's nothing more to say, we gaze down
at the floor, everything in a haze.
And nothing we can do but pray.
In the thick shadows below the ceiling,
I glimpse a disc the size of a frisbee;
some kind of miniature flying saucer
has entered the room. It drops slowly,
hovers above the hardwood, humming,
a diffuse light inches above the floor,
a red glow colouring an oblong shape below,
the humming loud as the sound of a truck
climbing a long and distant hill, the hum
hitting a crescendo, then gradually fading,
diminished, as soft as our breathing
now, the glow growing pale, dimming,
a sudden flicker, and the colour is done,
the disc itself wavering slightly, vanishing,
gone. We stare at the hardwood, bare
and cold. There's nothing we can do.

DEPARTURES

By now I should be expert at farewells
but life balks and rears, then gallops away

from goodbye. Colin shakes his head
when he sees me enter his room, a package

of brownies in my hand. No appetite,
he says, and we talk baseball instead.

Benton tells me it won't be long now
before he's back home; the next time

I visit there's a stranger in his bed.
Lorne and I strain to lift a makeshift porch roof

above his outside door. It will not fit.
Joan is feeling tired when we drop in,

her eyes drifting shut on casual chatter.
Flash and I laugh together, the old days

back again, polished bright as morning.
No way to know we're done, they

slip away without a chance to share
what I could only hope to say.

With Gary it's different. My hand
rubbing his left knee, "I love you, buddy,"

words that catch and collapse in my throat.
We both know that this is goodbye.

CENTRAL VAC

Monday afternoon, and I'm doing the vacuuming.
I've finished the living room, stretching to reach
under the sofa with its sprawl of hidden stereo wires,
poking at a bit of fluff snagged on the pad of a chair leg,
now pulling that long, long hose back through the hall,
across the kitchen floor and into the dining room,
swooping up crumbs under the dining room table

– a dark cluster, a clump of dried cereal, perhaps,
stuck tight on the floor by one table leg –

and over the hollow hum of the vacuum
I hear a click at the front door, the door
pushed open, and my wife's there

shaking her head, sorry she has to tell me
Colin is dead, and I feel the vacuum

sucking my breath away, or maybe
I just forget how to breathe,

I know he's in bad shape,
it might happen any day,

but not today, it can't
happen today.

TIME AND AGAIN

"The present, like your elbow, bends just one direction."
—Mark Cox in "Emergen(ce) of Feeling"

The past flings messages every which way. The ringing
of the alarm hauls you from sleep into a day that must be
grade five, the bully waiting just around the corner.
When you sit at the breakfast table slicing
a navel orange, juice sprays your glasses. Your vision
altered, you wipe the lens with a napkin, this morning
no more clear than last night's dream that churned
the covers off your bed. Waking at 3:00 am, you know
God is warning you to make a change. Consider
everything that's brought you here. Puddings
you ate when you might have chosen fruit.
The friend you never spoke to again.
Your memory huffs and puffs like the last
steam engine on the track. Now's the time
to get outside. Cats crapping in the flower bed,
cars at the next corner running the red light.
Wander a while. Two blocks down and another
to the right, a child sits on the curb, lifting
pebbles from the gutter, placing the shiny ones
in a row beside him, nodding and smiling as if
he has considered the meanings of life
and found satisfactory answers. Take
a hike, fella, was what that girl said fifty years ago,
but you, being you, had to hang around a while.
Some panes of glass are smeared with dirt
but even then they let the light shine through.
The rocking chair in the living room makes
your back ache; comfort is what you'll find

stretched out in your coffin. You often avoid
the best advice, and now you walk a while
in your own shoes, your aching feet bearing
you two blocks down. The choice is yours
always. You can bend the present any way
you want, but you must decide, the child
already grown, time plunging past.
Why not do it now?

SOMEWHERE OUT THERE

Some days I know I need a new friend, like Gary
beaming at poetry readings, Benton pouring
a tall rye and coke, Lorne walking the river valley,
or Colin talking Jays and the Jackie Robinson Dodgers,

but they're gone, the world bleaker
because they were here only a while.
I saw a movie once in which an old carpenter
confronts a young thug about to ransack his house.

Somehow the old guy decides to befriend him
and the two of them sit down and talk over coffee.
I don't know. I would've been on the phone to the cops
before he could warn me to shut my yap.

People would say I suffer from lack of trust,
but how can you trust a person you've never met?
There are strangers everywhere; some of them
enter convenience stores with knives in their hands.

Sometimes I linger in the public library, people
shoulder to shoulder at the magazine table,
a few seated in easy chairs, one of them
with a copy of *The New Yorker* spread on his knee.

Foolish is how I'd feel telling him to take a look
at page 73 as if a mutual love of cartoons
might bring us together. It's snowing outside,
the snow turning the lawn into a blank white page

where someone might write the name of a possible friend,
the snowflakes streaming now like crowds of shoppers,
Christmas around the corner, so many people
pushing by, and the streets are empty to me.

OMENS

There's a message that the years
have etched on my bones. Without reason
my back can seize me as if a mighty hand
is squeezing hard below the ribs, a warning
that any sudden move will shock me into spasms.

The signs are everywhere: in my eyes, for instance,
which will not recognize you half a block away
unless somehow you're stepping out the way
you used to step when even city streets were new,
arms swinging, hair tossed upon your shoulders,
the fervent bounce of youth that I remember
in your stride, and will not see again.

Reports arrive every time that I arise
from any chair in which I've sat too long,
my knees creaking, catches no lubricant can cure.
More and more, the daily paper brings the news,
another funeral I know I shouldn't miss,
an obituary almost every other day
of someone younger than myself.

Here's the outrage of the years:
most of the people I know
are dead. Damn the ravages of time
which pillages and plunders.
Another death holds its breath
and waits inside of me.

THE ONLY TICKET YOU'RE GIVEN

The ticket sewn into a patch on your jeans
like the name tag stitched under the collar
of an old man's shirt in the nursing home,
– you'd never know it's there, life heaped on your plate,
a meal you want to devour again and again.

The days ahead rush at you, greyhounds
after a mechanical rabbit, always a winner
to cheer for, the race on now and always,
you could run it yourself, your limbs
working like oiled pistons, but you discover
the ticket concealed in your jeans:
there might be an easier way.

Night falls, and you count on the new day,
as sure of it as of Sunday's roast beef dinner
– till your best friend drops at the office,
his heart stopped, change like a Freightliner truck
descending a hill, brakes failing, a curve ahead,
you at the bus stop just around the corner.
You've got that ticket you'd rather not use,
but departure might be safer than staying,
a crowd pushing to board, and why does
the ticket feel like cement in your pocket?

The driver says, Hold on, buddy,
this is a one-way ticket, you might
want to get off, but he's laughing at you,
shaking his head as the doors slam shut,
the bus rolling forward, and there isn't even
a seat at the back. You sway in the aisle,
wobbling with each bump and jerk, fighting
for balance, desperate to stay upright, dark
tunnel gaping ahead, the road narrow
and heaving, pavement broken.

ACKNOWLEDGEMENTS

Thanks to the editors of the following publications where some of these poems – occasionally in earlier versions – previously appeared: *CV2, Grain, Numero Cinq, Poetry Magazine.com, The Society 2017, The Society 2018, The Spadina Literary Review, An Amazing Eclectic Anthology* (Western Mountain Press, USA), *Line Dance* (Burton House Books), *Tamaracks: Canadian Poetry for the 21st Century* (Lummox Press, USA) and *Wilf Perreault: in the alley/dans la ruelle* (Coteau Books).

Special thanks to my editor, Dave Margoshes, for his patience, wisdom, and sound advice in turning the manuscript into a book. I also owe a lot to Byrna Barclay, Judith Krause, Katherine Lawrence, Jim McLean, Bruce Rice, and Paul Wilson for inspiration and helpful criticism over many years. Thanks, too, to Sheri Benning, Gary Hyland, Jeanette Lynes, Jim McLean, Brenda Niskala, and Joanne Weber for borrowed lines that inspired new poems and to Gerry Hill who instigated the Poetry Month project that led to those poems.

My gratitude goes as well to the Staff at Coteau, especially John Agnew, MacKenzie Hamon, and Susan Buck for their dedication and hard work, and to Wenda McArthur, Joanne Skidmore and the rest of the Coteau Board for keeping the publishing company afloat.

Additional thanks to Gwen Fisher and the staff of the Moose Jaw Public Library for their assistance and support. Also a tip of the hat to the staff and members of the Saskatchewan Writers' Guild whose support has been so important through the years.

ABOUT THE AUTHOR

Larry Hadwen

ROBERT CURRIE is a poet and fiction writer who lives in Moose Jaw, Saskatchewan where he taught for thirty years at Central Collegiate. His books have been finalists for the (now defunct) Commonwealth Poetry Prize, the Acorn-Plantos People's Poetry Award, the Poetry, Fiction, and Book of the Year Awards at the Saskatchewan Book Awards, and the High Plains Book Award for Poetry. A group of his poems was a winner in the 1980 CBC Literary Competition.

A founding board member of the Saskatchewan Festival of Words and a former chairman of the Saskatchewan Writers' Guild, Currie once edited and published *Salt*, a little magazine of contemporary writing. Highlights of his career include teaching creative writing at the Saskatchewan School of the Arts in Fort San and the Sage Hill Writing Experience in Lumsden, delivering the Anne Szumigalsaki Memorial Lecture for the League of Canadian poets, and serving two terms as Saskatchewan Poet Laureate. Currie is a recipient of the Saskatchewan Lieutenant Governor's Award for Lifetime Achievement in the Arts.

MIX
Paper from
responsible sources
FSC® C100212

Printed in September 2018
by Gauvin Press,
Gatineau, Québec